AF270743

This institution is dedicated

to the perpetual enjoyment, education, recreation

and cultural enlightenment

of the people of

the entire state of Tennessee.

Senator Albert Gore, Sr.
Sunday, May 22, 1960 Cheekwood Opening

CHEEKWOOD MUSEUM OF ART

COLLECTION CATALOG

EDITOR AND ESSAYIST: CELIA WALKER

WRITERS: KAYE CROUCH, KATIE DELMEZ, RUSTY FREEMAN, LISA PORTER, KARIN SACK, TERRI SMITH, JOHN WETENHALL

This collection catalogue could not have been created without the assistance of a number of people. The Cheekwood Board of Trustees and the Museum of Art Committee, led by chairs Jane Entrekin and Raymond White, approved funding for the project and showed enthusiastic support throughout its development. Jane Jerry, Cheekwood president, raised funds for the catalogue in the midst of a capital campaign. John Wetenhall, the museum's director, provided invaluable guidance at every step of the catalogue development. Kaye Crouch, the museum's registrar, oversaw the catalogue photography and provided technical information with Karin Sack, assistant registrar.

I would like to acknowledge the work of Beth Trabue, who organized the artists' photographs and contributed to two essays; Emily James and Nell Hodo, who assisted with research; photographers Greg Kinney and Lee Ewing; Archivist Wendy Hurlock, Archives of American Art; the Vanderbilt University Library staff and Cheekwood's own staff, past and present, whose research and effort led to this publication.

Celia Walker, Senior Curator

Cheekwood Museum of Art

---

editor and essayist: Celia Walker
creative director and front cover illustration: Buddy Jackson | Jackson Design
art direction, calligraphy and design: Karinne Miller Caulkins | Jackson Design
production manager: D. L. Rhodes | Jackson Design
copy editor: Bard Young
photographers: Greg Kinney and Lee Ewing
engraving: Colourworks, Jim Pomeroy
printing: TruColor

Published by Cheekwood Botanical Garden and Museum of art,
1200 Forrest Park Drive, Nashville, Tennessee, 37205

This catalogue was generously supported by the Henry Luce Foundation.

ISBN 0-9631349-3-0 Hardback   ISBN 0-9631349-4-9 Paperback
Library of Congress Catalogue Card Number 99-6478 "Formerly Cheekwood Tennessee Botanical Gardens and Museum of Art."

© Richard Cheek

UNLIKE THE GREAT OLD MUSEUMS OF THE NORTHEAST AND INDUSTRIAL MID-WEST, MOST SOUTHERN MUSEUMS ARE YOUNG, RELATIVELY NEWFOUND INSTITUTIONS. Lacking the expansive collections built through generations of acquisition, southern collections tend to evolve quickly, according to the generosity of local donors or the availability of funds as has happened here. Smaller size and a less established tradition can, however, have its advantages. A museum with vision can act to redefine itself, turning quickly to take advantage of opportunities. This happened at Cheekwood twice in recent times.

First, in the late 1980s the generous bequest of Anita Stallworth provided the museum with a major fund for the purchase of art. The trustees at the time concentrated new acquisitions on turn of the century painting, primarily to complement the holdings of other museums in Nashville. Over the following years, Cheekwood amassed quite a fine collection of paintings by the Eight. Second, in the late 1990s, Cheekwood undertook an $18 million capital campaign to pursue major improvements for its botanical gardens, to build a learning center with adjoining galleries for contemporary art, to create a woodland sculpture trail, and to restore the Cheek mansion to its original splendor. The sculpture trail, in particular, presented a monumental opportunity for acquiring and commissioning art that established Cheekwood as a premier facility for the display of world-class art in nature.

Southern taste for domestic elegance often accounts for fabulous examples of decorative arts and sometimes fine portraits. Cheekwood has been fortunate to receive substantial gifts from leaders in local taste. The Ewers-Tyne Worcester Porcelain collection, the Thompson Snuff Bottle collection, and the Caldwell silver collection all established core holdings around which an outstanding decorative arts collection could be established. Fine paintings came into the collection from a variety of donors. And the museum built significant collections of prints and photographs through its years of operation, especially through the Martin S. Ackerman Foundation gifts.

Southern museums have recently benefited from the extraordinary financial growth of the region. As southern cities began to enjoy a national profile, drawing in new residents attracted by business opportunities, lower prices, and a more livable pace of life, their museums thrived. New Orleans, Louisville, Savannah, Birmingham, Montgomery, and many other cities expanded their museums, often commissioning some of the finest architects in the country. Benefiting from the explosive growth of Nashville, now a new home to major league football and hockey franchises, a revitalized downtown, and a flourishing business environment, Cheekwood has enjoyed a similar boom.

For its first thirty-five years, then, Cheekwood's collections served a local house museum as much an historic mansion as a museum of art. The major improvements in the late 1990s expanded the institution to a regional level. The museum itself developed into three separate components: the fully renovated mansion with its paintings and decorative arts, a separate complex for the display of contemporary art, and a woodland sculpture trail featuring sculpture by some of the finest artists in the world. In raising the standards of our museum's operations, exhibitions, and permanent displays, this catalogue expands this effort toward scholarship, and stands as testimony to their dedication, knowledge, and extraordinary effort.

This catalogue marks yet another step in Cheekwood's development, this time as a museum ready to share its collection with a public beyond visitors to the site. Over the past four years, our curators and registrars have made extraordinary strides.

We must especially thank our senior curator, Celia Walker, for her vision, skill and perseverance in coordinating all facets of this catalogue's creation. We appreciate as well the support of our trustees, oversight committees, and the rest of the Cheekwood staff who made this project possible.

John Wetenhall, Ph.D.
Director, Cheekwood Museum of Art

Jane Jerry
President, Cheekwood Botanical Garden and Museum of Art

A Brief HISTORY of Cheekwood

RICHARD JACK (American, 1866-1952). *Portrait of Leslie Cheek, Sr.,* N.D. OIL ON CANVAS, GIFT OF MRS. WALTER SHARP. 1974.8.2

RAYMOND P.R. NEILSON. *Portrait of Mabel Cheek,* N.D. OIL ON CANVAS, GIFT OF MRS. WALTER SHARP. 1974.8.3

PHOTOGRAPH OF LESLIE, SR., HULDA AND MABEL CHEEK, EUROPEAN TOUR. CHEEKWOOD MUSEUM OF ART ARCHIVES. PHOTOGRAPHER UNKNOWN.

LIKE MANY AMERICAN MUSEUMS, CHEEKWOOD INITIALLY FUNCTIONED AS A PRIVATE RESIDENCE. Built during the Depression, the mansion and its surrounding one hundred acres were home to the Cheek family-father, Leslie, Sr.; mother, Mabel Wood Cheek (hence the name, "Cheekwood"); brother, Leslie, Jr.; and sister, Huldah. Leslie Cheek, Sr., came to Nashville from Kentucky in the late nineteenth century to work as a wholesale grocer. He also invested in his cousin Joel's coffee business, whose Maxwell House Coffee was named after the eponymous Nashville hotel. It was in this hotel that President Theodore Roosevelt reputedly declared the brew, "Good to the last drop!"

When Joel Cheek sold the coffee formula to Postum (later General Foods), he made his cousin Leslie a very wealthy man. Leslie had the business foresight to trade his Postum shares for IBM stock, a young company with which Leslie was probably familiar due to his work with cash registers at the grocery warehouse. With their finances thus secured, the Cheek family was prepared to build a stately residence. They promptly hired architect Bryant Fleming and sailed for Europe to purchase doors, mirrors, sconces, and other decorations for the new home.

"THE SHARPS ENTERTAIN AT NEW YEAR'S DAY RECEPTION AT CHEEKWOOD,"
The Nashville Tennessean, January 4, 1957. Photograph by Gerald Holly. Courtesy of the Nashville Tennessean.
Standing left to right: Mr. and Mrs. Walter Sharp, Mrs. Douglas Southall Freeman, Mr. and Mrs. Leslie Cheek, Jr.

"SCENE AT B.C. PARTY AT CHEEKWOOD TUESDAY NIGHT WHEN NASHVILLE SOCIETY IMPERSONATED
FAMOUS PERSONAGES OF ANCIENT WORLD, "The Nashville Banner, July 15, 1934, Second Section. Photograph by Commerical Photograph Company.
Courtesy of Nashville Public Library Banner Archives Collection. Members of the receiving party, standing left to right: Mrs. Louis Wood, representing Ceres; Combs Fort, Zephyr;
Helen Bersbach of Winnetka, Ill., Aurora; Briggs McLemore, Aeolus; Barbara Bersbach of Winnetka, Flora, Allen Bryan, Jason; Sally Coburn of Reading, Pa., Medea; Mrs. Cheek, Juno; Mr. Cheek, Jupiter;
Huldah Cheek, Athena; and William Steel of Philadelphia, Mars

Photograph of BRYANT FLEMING, Architect of Cheek mansion. Cheekwood Museum of Art Archives. Photographer unknown.

PREPARATORY PLANS FOR THE MANSION EVOLVED ACROSS A CONTINENT OF TASTE: FIRST, SPANISH STYLE, THEN A FRENCH PLAN, UNTIL THE FAMILY FINALLY AGREED UPON A NEO-GEORGIAN DESIGN, BASED UPON EIGHTEENTH-CENTURY BRITISH ARCHITECTURE. The Cheeks utilized several woodwork and masonry elements from England, including a Robert Adam mantel inlaid with lapis lazuli and mahogany-and-fruitwood doors from Grosvenor House in London. Continuing this British influence, the mansion's main floor rotunda was based on the designs of Sir Christopher Wren; trompe l'oeil panels from the seventeenth-century were placed in the adjacent transverse hallway. On Thanksgiving day, 1932, the Cheeks moved into the nearly completed stables complex, and by January of 1933 they were settled into the thirty-six room mansion.

MEMBERS OF THE CHEEK FAMILY CONTINUED TO LIVE IN THE MANSION UNTIL 1959, WHEN HULDAH CHEEK SHARP AND HER HUSBAND, WALTER SHARP, GRACIOUSLY DEEDED THE MANSION AND FIFTY-FIVE ACRES TO THE CHEEKWOOD FINE ARTS CENTER. The Sharp's gift was conditional upon the Center's ability to raise $200,000 to pay for necessary renovations and three years of operating expenses. This was accomplished through the help of countless individual donors as well as three local organizations: the Nashville Exchange Club, the Horticulture Society of Davidson County, and the Nashville Museum of Art.

The Nashville Museum of Art's donation to Cheekwood is particularly noteworthy. In 1960 the museum sold its West End Avenue building and gave the proceeds and the bulk of its art collection to the newly established Cheekwood Center. Previously, the Nashville Museum of Art had traced its roots to the Nashville Art Association, founded in 1883 by prominent Nashvillians. Its purpose had been to foster "the art interests of the city and state, [and] the creating and encouraging [of] advanced schools of the fine arts." To that end, the Association held numerous exhibitions, lectures, and classes and formed a sizable collection of art. The institution went through a series of name changes, eventually becoming the Nashville Museum of Art in 1926.

Utilizing the $55,000 donation from the Nashville Museum of Art, the Cheekwood Center set about making a series of much-needed improvements to the physical plant. During the winter of 1959, the museum hired Nashville architects Street & Street to create lighted galleries on the center's second floor. In addition, the house was air conditioned, and parking facilities were created for visitors. Harry Lowe was hired to become the Fine Arts Center's first director, and the Center itself opened to the public on May 22, 1960, with two exhibitions on display: *Tennessee Painting-The Past* and *Tennessee Artists Now*. At this opening, Senator Albert Gore, Sr., accepted a key to Cheekwood and dedicated the property "to the perpetual enjoyment, education, recreation and cultural enlightenment of the people of the entire state of Tennessee." During a productive first year, the Fine Arts Center curated fourteen exhibits and added over forty new acquisitions to the Center's permanent collection. In 1961 Mr. Lowe began the popular series *Your Neighbors Collect*, which continued for five years and proved a valuable source for donations to the collection.

"GIRL FRIDAYS AID CHEEKWOOD," *THE NASHVILLE TENNESSEAN*, APRIL 26, 1959. PHOTOGRAPH BY ELDRED REANEY. COURTESY OF *THE NASHVILLE TENNESSEAN*. MRS. HORACE G. HILL, JR. AND OTHER GARDEN CLUB MEMBERS AWAIT THE OPENING OF CHEEKWOOD.

The series presented a wide range of genres, including paintings, portraits, decorative arts, birds, and floral motifs. Highlights of the loaned exhibits from this period included a retrospective of David Park's contemporary art from the Oakland Art Museum (1962), *Benjamin West: An American Abroad* from the Museum of Fine Arts, Boston (1963), and an exhibit of Yugoslavian frescoes organized by the Smithsonian Institution (1965).

Mr. Lowe left Cheekwood in 1964 to become Curator of Exhibits for the National Collection of Fine Arts at the Smithsonian Institution. B. Charles Elliott, Jr., served as director for one year, followed by donor Walter Sharp, who served as acting director for the next three years. By 1965, the Center was confident enough in its progress to exhibit *One Hundred Works from the Permanent Collection,* the first time in which the galleries had been filled with objects from the permanent collection alone. In 1968, under the leadership of new director Russell MacBeth, Cheekwood organized the exhibit *Tennessee Painting Today*, a follow-up to the Center's inaugural shows. It included the work of forty Tennessee artists and traveled the state for two years.

WALTER SHARP AND PURYEAR MIMS PREPARE AN EXHIBIT AT THE PARTHENON. Cheekwood Museum of Art Archives. Photographer unknown.

PHOTOGRAPH OF HARRY LOWE, THE MUSEUM'S FIRST DIRECTOR. *The Nashville Banner*, May 23, 1960, p. 29. Photograph by Tim Harden. Courtesy of Nashville Public Library *Banner* Archives Collection.

The Center celebrated its tenth birthday in May of 1970 with an exhibition of recent acquisitions and a lecture by noted art historian Robert Rosenblum, sponsored by the newly established Walter Sharp Distinguished Lectureship. Mr. MacBeth took the opportunity to review the Center's mission in a special-edition member newsletter, which highlighted the important role of the Center as a resource for unique, object-based edification of children and adults. His last exhibit before leaving for the Gibbes Art Gallery in Charleston, South Carolina, was *Tennessee Sculpture 1971*, an exhibit organized by the Chattanooga Art Association. His successor, twenty-seven-year-old John Nozynski, became director of the Center in 1972. *The Cheekwood Mirror* listed his interests as "ceramics, weaving … and prints" and noted that he "had established bachelor quarters" in the Cheekwood gatehouse.

Mr. Nozynski spearheaded many new programs at Cheekwood. He instituted study groups for collectors, began a film series, organized art tours, and encouraged the Nashville Artists' Guild to locate their headquarters at the Center. The Guild took over two rooms on the main floor of the mansion for member exhibits, across from the art sales gallery. In 1973 the Center exhibited the *Tennessee Painting and Sculpture Exhibition*, a competition bringing together eighty-four works of art, which was sponsored by Commerce Union Bank. The same exhibit was shown again in 1976 in celebration of the country's bicentennial. Mr. Nozynski revived the series *Your Neighbors Collect* in 1973 with the exhibition *American Survey-Turn of the Century Your Neighbors Collect*. Other exhibits were composed of paintings that the Center hoped to acquire from New York dealers. Local art patrons were encouraged to buy artworks from the shows and to promise to give them to the Center at some future date. In early 1977 Jamie Wyeth and Andy Warhol came to Cheekwood for the opening of the exhibition *Andy Warhol and Jamie Wyeth: Portraits of Each Other*. The museum's subsequent purchase of two works from the exhibit made national news.

 Committees undertook the planning of period rooms in the mansion's silver library and drawing room. In 1978 a $2,000,000 fund drive was launched to expand the galleries, move the tea room out of the mansion, and add sprinkler and security systems in anticipation of application for American Association of Museums accreditation. The last exhibit prior to closing for the renovation was in October 1979-*The Permanent Collection Show*, which highlighted outstanding work in the permanent collection.

During this time of renovation, Kevin Grogan came to Cheekwood as director from the Phillips Collection in Washington, D.C., in January 1980. That year, the mansion's service wing was converted into the Anita Stallworth Galleries, named for one of Cheekwood's greatest benefactors. Electronic security and sprinkler systems were installed

L-R PHOTOGRAPH OF SUSAN KNOWLES, KEVIN GROGAN AND LOUISE DAHL-WOLFE (SEATED). CHEEKWOOD MUSEUM OF ART ARCHIVES. PHOTOGRAPHER UNKNOWN.

PHOTOGRAPH OF DR. JOHN WETENHALL AT THE REOPENING OF CHEEKWOOD MUSEUM, 1999. CHEEKWOOD MUSEUM OF ART ARCHIVES. PHOTOGRAPHER UNKNOWN.

and new storage and workspace areas added in the Center. The ground floor gift shop was converted to staff offices. A modified exhibit schedule was carried out in the Botanic Hall. The Center reopened to the public in May 1981 with *A Collector's Eye: The Olga Hirshhorn Collection*, along with a commitment to a continuing series of media-specific exhibits and to the display of work by artists from the Southeast.

Over the next ten years, Mr. Grogan parlayed his connections with the Washington, D.C., art world and took advantage of Tennesseans' growing interest in art to produce numerous diverse exhibits in the new space. An aggressive acquisition program for Worcester porcelain was led by Mrs. William J. Tyne in her role as chair of the Decorative Arts Committee. The Center's name was changed to the Cheekwood Museum of Art to reflect the institution's interests in fine and decorative arts. In an effort to encourage public attendance, the museum offered free admission on Tuesday afternoons and launched a concert series.

By 1991 Cheekwood's membership had risen to nine thousand. In that same year the museum held the first of a series of five national contemporary painting competitions. Jurors for the competitions included such distinguished artists as Kenneth Noland and Nashville native Robert Ryman. A generous bequest from the estate of Anita Stallworth was used in part to purchase approximately forty works by the Eight, a group of early urban realists important to the development of the modern movement in America.

Since 1995, the Cheekwood Museum of Art has expanded its exhibition programming under the leadership of Dr. John Wetenhall. The number of exhibits has been reduced and more time has been put into planning programs for the shows. A web site was developed to expand educational outreach and to provide international access to the museum and its collections. Highlights of the Museum of Art's recent exhibition program have included: *William H. Johnson: A Retrospective, The Huguenot Legacy, Dorothea Lange, and African-American Art from the Walter O. Evans Collection,* all part of the institution's ongoing effort to diversify its offerings and expand its audience. The critically acclaimed *Temporary Contemporary* series, begun in 1995, offers monthly shows by regional artists to provide a resource for viewing outstanding Southern art. In 1996 the museum originated the blockbuster exhibition, *Andrew Wyeth: The Olson Saga,* which brought internationally renowned artwork to Nashville, won the Tennessee Association of Museums' "Award of Excellence," and broke Cheekwood attendance records. Dr. Wetenhall also created the Carell Woodland Sculpture Trail (which opened in June 1999) to display world-class sculpture in Cheekwood's unique natural setting. The participation of renowned artists such as George Rickey, Ulrich Ruckriem, Ian Hamilton Finlay,

SOPHIE RYDER, *Crawling Lady Hare, 1997*, GALVANIZED WIRE ON STEEL ARMATURE, MUSEUM PURCHASE, 1997.8

Sophie Ryder, Doug Hollis, John Scott, Eric Orr, and James Turrell has provided Cheekwood an international presence in the art community.

In November of 1998, the Museum's Contemporary Collection was placed in new galleries in the recently renovated and expanded Frist Learning Center. And in August 1999 the Museum of Art completed its third renovation of the Cheek home, bringing back the best aspects of the original mansion with main-floor furnishings that reflect the original function of the building. Display areas have been redesigned with ramps to provide wheelchair access to many previously inaccessible areas. Upgraded security, climate control, and storage and receiving areas give Cheekwood the opportunity to bring in traveling exhibits of the highest quality, and newly installed fiber-optic cables allow us to interpret the works utilizing the most advanced technology available from the World Wide Web. Mixing the past with the present, improvements and additions will allow the museum to sail smoothly into the twenty-first century.

A Brief HISTORY of the COLLECTION

LILLIAN GENTH, *Summer Afternoon,* c. 1910, oil on canvas, Transfer from the Nashville Museum of Art 1960.2.36

Epergne, 1865, sterling silver, Gift of Mrs. Walter Sharp, 1983.5.4–7

FLIGHT (ENGLISH, ACTIVE 1783–1792), *Dish,* c. 1785, Royal lily pattern, porcelain, Gift of Dr. and Mrs. Benjamin Caldwell, Jr. , 1991.7

DONATIONS TO CHEEKWOOD'S COLLECTION BEGAN ARRIVING IN 1957, SOON AFTER MR. AND MRS. WALTER SHARP DONATED THE ART CENTER. Still undergoing minor renovation, the Cheek's family home would not open to the public for three more years. The first large gift to the collection was a group of 350 Asian snuff bottles, donated by Mr. and Mrs. Joseph H. Thompson in honor of Mr. Thompson's mother, Mrs. Willie DeMoville Thompson. Additional donations by the Thompson family later increased the size and variety of this collection to over six hundred objects.

The young museum's collection of fine art grew quickly with the 1960 donation of the majority of the Nashville Museum of Art's permanent collection, which contained over six hundred objects, including over seventy paintings, two hundred drawings, and three hundred prints, along with forty-three china objects. Most of that museum's purchases had been made from a fund established by the Nashville Art Association's second president, General Gates P. Thruston, a Federal general in the Civil War who participated in the Battle of Nashville.

RALPH E. W. EARL, *The Ephraim Hubbard Foster Family,* C. 1825, OIL ON MATTRESS TICKING, GIFT OF MRS. JOSEPHUS DANIELS, 1969.2

Earlier acquisitions by the Nashville Museum of Art had favored European paintings in the then-popular style of the old masters but also included genre subjects, landscapes, and portraits by American artists. Some European porcelain had been acquired, as well as commemorative plaster studies for war memorials and European plaques. Works in this catalogue by Lillian Genth, Edgar J. Bissell, John Wood Dodge, and Julian Story came to the Cheekwood collection from the Nashville Museum of Art.

DURING THE 1960S AND 1970S CHEEKWOOD ACCEPTED MOST OFFERED OBJECTS SO THAT BY 1980 THE MUSEUM HAD TRIPLED THE SIZE OF THE ORIGINAL NASHVILLE MUSEUM OF ART GIFT. Cheekwood's collection of limestone sculpture by William Edmondson was begun in 1960 with the gift of an Edmondson statue of a schoolteacher from John Thompson, Jr. In a period when work by untrained artists was underappreciated, director Harry Lowe's decision to collect in this area showed great vision. With major donations by Elizabeth Lyle Starr, Mr. and Mrs. Thompson, and the Formosa family, and with purchases made through a bequest by Anita Stallworth, Cheekwood's holdings would grow over the next three decades into the nation's largest Edmondson collection.

CHEEKWOOD'S PHOTOGRAPHY COLLECTION ALSO GOT ITS START IN THE 1960S WITH A LARGE GIFT OF LOUISE DAHL-WOLFE FASHION PHOTOGRAPHS FROM THE ARTIST HERSELF. In the 1980s Dahl-Wolfe would make additional donations to the collection of her own silver prints and of paintings and sculpture by her artist/husband, Meyer Wolfe. The photography collection at Cheekwood would greatly expand in the 1980s when the Martin S. Ackerman Foundation facilitated the donation of a series of photographs by Berenice Abbott, Philippe Halsman, George Hurrell, Barbara Morgan, and Eugene Smith, and also donated a large number of Victorian travel photographs.

Other large donations of the 1960s were international in scope: for instance, the ethnographic collection donated by the Rufus Fort family and a large number of Japanese prints from Mr. and Mrs. Russell Speights were received at that time. The ethnographic collection would grow in 1972 with a gift of African objects from Mr. and Mrs. John Connally and again in 1977 when the Forts and Dr. and Mrs. Benjamin Caldwell donated a collection of African pieces. Important contemporary American prints would enter the collection through donations by Mr. and Mrs. Walter Sharp, Cheekwood's largest benefactors, from Dr. and Mrs. Caldwell, and through purchases made during the early 1970s. Again through the donations of the Ackerman Foundation, the print collection at Cheekwood would grow dramatically in the 1980s. Between 1981 and 1984 over one thousand prints were received in the collection, most of which were created by contemporary British printmakers. The museum organized several traveling exhibits of the prints, earning income and publicizing the institution.

Donations to the painting collection slowed during the 1960s with the exception of an Isabel Bishop painting and several fine regional paintings by Cornelius Hankins and Ella Hergesheimer. In the 1970s, activity increased with the purchase of the anonymous Cheat River Gorge and individual donations of paintings by Childe Hassam, John Singer Sargent, Ernest Lawson, Frank Duveneck, and William Merritt Chase. In addition, the Walter Sharps donated family portraits of Mabel Wood Cheek and Leslie Cheek.

IN THE 1980S THREE LARGE GIFTS FROM MR. AND MRS. WALTER KNESTRICK GREATLY ENHANCED THE HOLDINGS OF THE PAINTING COLLECTION. These gifts included paintings by George Luks, Julian Alden Weir, William Merritt Chase, Frank Duveneck, Eastman Johnson, George Inness, Thomas Sully, Samuel F. B. Morse, Rembrandt and James Peale, Ernest Lawson, Guy Péne du Bois, and many others. The paintings were supported by drawings by Charles Burchfield, Everett Shinn, Robert Henri, Maurice Prendergast, John Singer Sargent, and Alfred Maurer. The paintings by Luks and Lawson together with these drawings would form the basis for the museum's collection of works by the Eight. Important additions to that collection by William Glackens, Maurice Prendergast, Everett Shinn, Arthur B. Davies, Robert Henri, Ernest Lawson, George Luks, and John Sloan were made possible in the 1990s by the Anita Stallworth bequest and Collectors' Group funds.

WILLIAM BRADFORD, *Sunset in the Arctic,* N.D., OIL ON CANVAS, GIFT OF MR. HANS ANDERSEN, 1998.11.3

WILLIAM EDMONDSON, *Eve,* C. 1930S, LIMESTONE, GIFT OF MRS. ALFRED STARR, 1964.10

CRAFTSMAN UNKNOWN, CHINESE *Snuff Bottle,* 18TH CENTURY, GLASS, GIFT OF MRS. JOSEPH THOMPSON, 1958.1.126

CHARLES (RED) GROOMS, *Mr. and Mrs. Rembrandt,* C. 1971, WOOD, FABRIC AND FOUND MATERIALS, GIFT OF MR. AND MRS. ERVIN M. ENTREKIN AND MR. AND MRS. WALTER KNESTRICK, 1975.9.8

In the late 1950s Mrs. Hugh Stallworth was one of the prime organizers of Cheekwood, and she continued to support the institution throughout her lifetime. She served on the board of the Nashville Museum of Art, Cheekwood's predecessor, and for six years as its president. Several important paintings in Cheekwood's collection were gifts of Anita Stallworth, including works by Frank Duveneck, Martha Walter, Ernest Lawson, and A. C. Goodwin. Mrs. Stallworth was also a donor toward the 1976 purchase of paintings by Andy Warhol and Jamie Wyeth. Many of the museum's porcelain objects came from Mrs. Stallworth's collection. She also supported museum exhibitions, publications, and staff development-important areas less likely to attract donor support. In 1980 she donated funds to convert the mansion's service area into galleries that today bear her name. After her death in 1986, her bequest to the museum allowed Cheekwood to complete its collection of works by the Eight. Funds from Mrs. Stallworth were also used to renovate the mansion in the late 1990s, making it climate controlled, secure, and more accessible to the public.

The Failure of Sylvester, 1914, oil on canvas, Museum Purchase through the bequest of Anita Bevill McMichael Stallworth, 1993.6

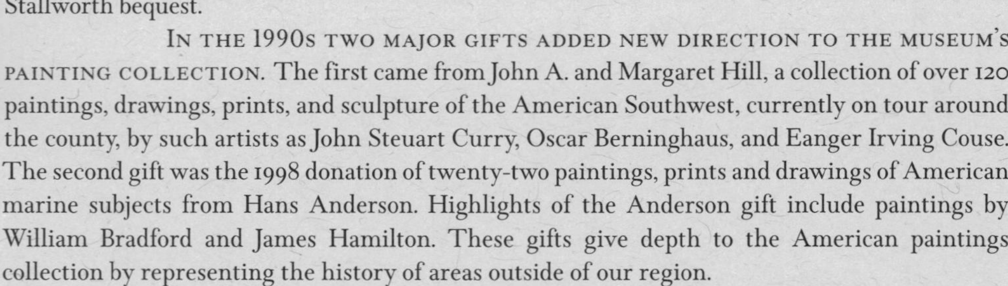

Over the years Cheekwood acquired many works by twentieth-century Tennessee artists, including the aforementioned Meyer Wolfe collection, a large group of paintings by Cornelius Hankins, drawings by Nashville natives A. C. Webb and Werner Wildner, and works from the estate of Eugene Biel-Bienne. A small but growing collection of works by Nashville native Red Grooms has been acquired over the years, highlighted by Grooms's picto-sculpto-rama *Mr. and Mrs. Rembrandt,* donated by Mr. and Mrs. Ervin Entrekin and Mr. and Mrs. Walter Knestrick. These works augmented a strong group of nineteenth-century Tennessee paintings, featuring the spectacular *The Ephraim Hubbard Foster Family,* by Ralph E. W. Earl, donated by Mrs. Josephus Daniels. During the late 1980s Dr. A. Everett James, Jr., donated paintings by Gilbert Gaul, Robert Loftin Newman, and Washington Girard that strengthened this regional collection. Paintings by Newman, Ella Hergesheimer, and Thomas Waterman Wood were purchased in the late 1980s through the Stallworth bequest.

In the 1990s two major gifts added new direction to the museum's painting collection. The first came from John A. and Margaret Hill, a collection of over 120 paintings, drawings, prints, and sculpture of the American Southwest, currently on tour around the county, by such artists as John Steuart Curry, Oscar Berninghaus, and Eanger Irving Couse. The second gift was the 1998 donation of twenty-two paintings, prints and drawings of American marine subjects from Hans Anderson. Highlights of the Anderson gift include paintings by William Bradford and James Hamilton. These gifts give depth to the American paintings collection by representing the history of areas outside of our region.

In 1960 the decorative arts at Cheekwood were represented by the Thompson collection of Asian snuff bottles and approximately fifty pieces of china from the Nashville Museum of Art. The Cheekwood Museum's silver collection got its start in 1970 with a large gift of Sheffield silver from Mr. and Mrs. Russell Speights. The Speights made additional gifts to the collection in 1981, and in 1991 Dr. and Mrs. Benjamin Caldwell donated a large grouping of American and British silver to the museum, including a meat cover by Paul Storrs.

During the 1970s Mr. and Mrs. George Ware and the Walter Sharps donated gifts of glass and furniture, respectively. Limitations of space inside the mansion, however, have necessarily restricted further acquisition of fine furniture and indoor sculpture. Mr. and Mrs. Allen O. Mason donated twenty-three examples of Tiffany and art nouveau glass in 1995, creating a small but growing collecting area. That same year Mrs. Thomas K. Connor donated her late husband's collection of thirty-two brass candlesticks.

In 1978 the Ewers Acquisition Fund was established for the purchase of Worcester porcelain. Two benefactresses, Marge Ewers and Harriet Tyne, spearheaded the collection, which grew to become one of the largest of its kind in

JAMIE WYETH AND ANDY WARHOL AT THE FACTORY, ©PETER BEARD

the United States. Over the course of the 1980s and early 1990s, these women aggressively sought donations and funds to build the collection, which contains a large number of armorial pieces. Henry Sandon served as advisor to the collection during those years, and many objects were purchased through the Stallworth bequest.

The creation of the Carell Woodland Sculpture Trail in the late 1990s opened a new setting for Cheekwood's collection. Using funds donated by Mr. and Mrs. Monroe Carell as part of Cheekwood's $18 million capital campaign, the museum's director, John Wetenhall, commissioned pieces by some of the finest sculptors in the world and, thereby, set out to establish Cheekwood as a major venue for the display of outdoor sculpture. Sophie Ryder from England, Eric Orr from Los Angeles, John Scott of New Orleans, Siah Armajani of Minneapolis, and James Turrell of Arizona were recruited to design monumental, site-specific sculptures for the trail. In addition, major pieces by such world-class sculptors as Ulrich Ruckriem, Ian Hamilton Finlay, Doug Hollis, and George Rickey were acquired, endowing Cheekwood with a collection of outdoor sculpture that is, though relatively small, widely recognized as one of the finest in the country.

The Cheekwood staff and the Museum of Art Committee regularly review the more than seven thousand objects in the museum's collection in the light of collecting goals. Objects that do not relate to the museum's goals are deaccessioned during the process, and funds from those sales are used to purchase additional art works in the original donors' names. Today, the museum continues to collect American fine art, contemporary art, silver, Worcester porcelain, and glass.

DETAIL: MILTON RESNICK (American, B. 1917) *Untitled,* 1958, OIL ON PAPER, GIFT OF GRACE BORGENICHT BRANDT, 1984.21.21

There are moments in our lives,

there are moments in a day,

when we seem to see beyond the usual.

Such are the moments

of our greatest happiness.

Such are the moments of our greatest wisdom.

Robert Henri, The Art Spirit, 1923

There are moments in our lives,
there are moments in a day,
when we seem to see beyond the usual.
Such are the moments
of our greatest happiness.
Such are the moments of our greatest wisdom.

Robert Henri, The Art Spirit, 1923

GILBERT STUART (AMERICAN, 1755–1828),
Portrait of an Unknown Gentleman (possibly General Pierson), N.D., OIL ON CANVAS, GIFT OF
MR. AND MRS. WALTER KNESTRICK, 1986.16.23
EVEN THOUGH STUART WAS CONSIDERED A GREAT PAINTER
IN EUROPE, NOT ALL PATRONS WANTED SUCH REALISTIC
PORTRAYALS OF THEMSELVES. CRITICS OFTEN CONSIDERED
STUART'S WORK TOO HARSH, WHICH GENERALLY LIMITED
HIS SUBJECTS TO MEN, THOUGHT BETTER SUITED TO HIS
STYLE. IN AMERICA, HOWEVER, STUART'S REALISM
APPEALED TO BOTH MALE AND FEMALE CLIENTS, WHO FELT
HIS STYLE APPROPRIATE TO DEMOCRATIC SOCIETY.

ATTRIBUTED TO GILBERT STUART
(AMERICAN, 1755–1828), *Portrait of George
Washington*, N.D., OIL ON CANVAS, GIFT OF THE
ESTATE OF NANCY W. HOWELL, 1998.1
THIS PORTRAIT IS BASED ON STUART'S FAMOUS
ATHENÆUM PORTRAIT OF GEORGE WASHINGTON,
WHICH IS CONSIDERED ONE OF STUART'S MOST
ARTISTICALLY SUCCESSFUL PORTRAITS. HAVING
RECEIVED AN OVERWHELMING NUMBER OF REQUESTS FOR
COPIES, HE SPENT MUCH OF HIS LATER CAREER PAINTING
DUPLICATES. STUART'S *ATHENÆUM* PORTRAIT WAS
LATER ENGRAVED FOR USE ON THE ONE-DOLLAR BILL.

GILBERT STUART, *Self-Portrait*
THE TATE GALLERY, LONDON, 2000

GILBERT STUART (AMERICAN, 1755–1828)

From the beginning of his career, Gilbert Stuart focused on painting portrait busts, rarely deviating into other kinds of portraiture. In head and shoulder views, Stuart found he could describe the sitter's personality through facial features and simple gestures without the distracting, busy backdrops and surrounding accoutrements typical of larger portraits. *The Portrait of William McCracken* exemplifies Stuart's genius for achieving a realistic likeness of his sitter while recording the subject with dignity, intelligence, and inner being. William McCracken, a bishop from Dublin, was painted to commemorate his part in founding the first Sunday school program in Belfast. He holds a letter in his hand that reads, "Since then we can no longer have yr. [your] presence as usual permit us to request a Memento to remind us of him who has been The Father of our Schools."

Discovered by Scottish portrait painter Cosimo Alexander (c. 1724–1772), Stuart traveled with Alexander as his pupil through the American colonies and later to Scotland. Shortly after they arrived in Scotland, Alexander died, and soon after Stuart made passage back to America to open his own studio. Not satisfied with his work, he sailed again to Great Britain with the help of relatives. In London Stuart struggled for some years on his own before Benjamin West, a renowned American painter, accepted Stuart into his studio. Stuart completed his training with West and became acquainted with many influential British painters, such as Sir Joshua Reynolds and Thomas Gainsborough. He worked in West's studio with such distinguished American painters as John Singleton Copley and John Trumbull. Stuart shortly mastered not only Benjamin West's style but also the fluid brush stroke of Sir Joshua Reynolds, the preeminent British portrait painter at the time.

Before leaving West's studio to work on his own, Stuart defined his own sense of color, unlike that of any of his peers. According to biographer Charles Blount, Benjamin West once noted to his other apprentices: "It's no use to steal Stuart's colors. If you want to paint as he does you must steal his eyes." Stuart also departed from tradition by skipping preliminary drawings. Stuart felt that drawings produced a hard-edged, linear appearance and slowed down the painting process. Instead, he rubbed-in a circular area of flesh tones with his brush on which he built up facial features with paint. Stuart not only attained the softness and tactility of flesh using this method, but his portraits achieved a likeness more genuine and accurate than that achieved by any rival painters. Patrons were not only impressed by Stuart's realism; they also admired his ability to convey the inner spirit of the sitter.

Portrait painting for most artists in the eighteenth century was not profitable enough to justify exclusive concentration. The typical artist's greatest source of revenue came from the sale of engravings based on original works of art. For financial success, paintings had to appeal to engravers who could then circulate image reproductions through the marketplace. Engravers sought history paintings, while Stuart produced portraits that rarely interested them. In addition to Stuart's financial problems, he was unable to say "no" to clients; thus, he struggled to keep up with the demand for his work, leaving many projects unfinished. In 1787 Stuart, forced to leave London due to extensive debts, moved to Dublin. By 1793 debts again forced him to leave for North America, where he achieved his greatest fame painting portraits of George Washington. American clientele embraced Stuart's realism, prompting him to remark, "In England my efforts were compared with those of Van Dyck, Titian, and other great painters—here they are compared with the works of the Almighty."

Portrait of William McCracken, N.D., OIL ON CANVAS, GIFT OF MR. AND MRS. WALTER KNESTRICK, 1989.3.2

The Ephraim Hubbard Foster Family, c. 1825, oil on mattress ticking, Gift of Mrs. Josephus Daniels, 1969.2

RALPH ELEASER WHITESIDE EARL (AMERICAN, 1785–1838)

Nashville in the early 1820s was transforming from the frontier settlement founded at Fort Nashborough by James Robertson in 1779 to the bustling center of commerce it would become by mid-century. While the census of 1800 paints Nashville as a small town of only four-hundred inhabitants, by 1819 Nashville reported three-thousand residents. Also in that year, the first steamboat, the General Jackson, reached Nashville from New Orleans. The steamboat's arrival marked the beginning of a new era for the town, for it was by water that most goods and services would come to Nashville.

Ephraim Foster understood the importance of the Cumberland River: it appears in the distance in this family portrait of around 1825. Without it, the fine Empire chairs on which Colonel and Mrs. Foster sit, the fringed red draperies that adorn their window, and the feathered French hat worn by baby Jane Foster would probably never have made it to Nashville. Still, goods were scarce in town, as evidenced by the artist's having painted his subjects on mattress ticking instead of canvas.

Ralph E. W. Earl studied under his father, the New England portrait painter Ralph Earl, and became known as "the king's painter" for his numerous portraits of President Andrew Jackson. Earl became so close to Jackson that he was buried in the cemetery of Jackson's Nashville home, the Hermitage.

By the time that Earl painted this portrait, Col. Ephraim Hubbard Foster had already established himself as private secretary to Gen. Andrew Jackson, having served Jackson during the Creek War of 1813–1815 at the battles of Talledega, Enoctochopee, Emuefaw, and Topeka. In 1817 Foster married Jane Dickinson, the widow of the attorney for whom he apprenticed. Foster was admitted to the bar in 1820 and developed a thriving practice. Foster was known for his wit and his temper, so unrestrained that a story from 1821 has him throwing a book at a local judge during trial.

Ralph Earl's portrait shows Foster at one of the high points of his life. He is about thirty-five years old, surrounded by his wife and five children (John, the boy behind Ephraim, was the son of Jane's first husband; Colonel Foster adopted him). Earl portrayed the Fosters as a well-to-do family in expensive apparel and elegant furnishings, quite unlike the typical accommodations of 1825 Nashville. Yet he made the family real to us by adding personal touches, such as the penny whistle in the young girl's hand and the outrageous hat that Jane Dickinson has indulgently allowed her young daughter to wear. All members of the family are embracing, holding or touching each other while the baby in his mother's lap has been depicted sucking his fingers. Incidentally, the baby was born while the portrait was being completed and was added later, as indicated by the way the child's contours follow the folds of the mother's dress.

Although Colonel Foster would go on to greater achievements (serving in the U.S. Senate and as Speaker of the House), his successes would be tempered with sadness—the loss of his wife in 1847 and, later, of his two grown daughters. Colonel Foster became estranged from Andrew Jackson, whose well-documented violent temper would inevitably collide with Foster's own hot head. In the late 1830s Foster devoted himself to keeping Texas out of the union. His failure, and the public protests he voiced, became his political undoing.

RALPH E. W. EARL (AMERICAN, 1785–1838), *Portrait of Brigadier Robert Coleman Foster,* N.D., OIL ON CANVAS, BEQUEST OF MR. STRATTON M. FOSTER, 1985.4.1 IN THIS PORTRAIT EARL PAINTED EPHRAIM FOSTERS' FATHER, ROBERT.

ATTRIBUTED TO WASHINGTON BOGART COOPER (AMERICAN, 1802–1889), *Ephraim Hubbard Foster,* C. 1860, OIL ON CANVAS, GIFT OF THE ESTATE OF MR. STRATTON M. FOSTER, 1985.4.2 ESSENTIALLY SELF-TAUGHT, COOPER MANAGED A THRIVING PORTRAIT BUSINESS IN TENNESSEE IN THE MID-NINETEENTH CENTURY AND PAINTED MANY OF THE STATE'S OFFICIALS.

JAMES PEALE (AMERICAN, 1749–1831),
Portrait of Judge Trimble, N.D., OIL ON CANVAS,
GIFT OF MR. AND MRS. WALTER KNESTRICK, 1985.29.8

 24   paintings

One of the most celebrated painters of his time, Charles Willson Peale (1741–1827) raised his children from the crib to be artists: he named them after Renaissance and other master artists–Raphael, Rembrandt, Rubens, and Titian. Rembrandt was his father's favorite, perhaps the most talented of the brothers and certainly the most ambitious. He trained under his father, one of the few first-generation American artists to study in London. Rembrandt Peale's early style shows his father's influence in its simplified palette and modeling. To boost his son's career, the elder Peale convinced George Washington to allow Rembrandt, then only seventeen years old, to paint the famous American's portrait. The subject would eventually become Rembrandt's main source of income. In the meantime, he made a good living painting portraits of the Philadelphia upper class.

Charles Willson Peale sent his son to England in 1802 to study with Benjamin West. The time spent overseas allowed Rembrandt to develop a more sophisticated, painterly style, as taught by West and by West's own teacher, Sir Joshua Reynolds. West encouraged Peale to paint historical subjects instead of the portraits that had been the source of his income. West wrote to Peale's father,

> *Although I am friendly to portraying eminent men, I am not friendly to the indiscriminate waste of genius in portrait painting and I hope that your son will ever bear this in mind, that the art of painting has powers to dignify man, by transmitting to posterity his noble actions, and his mental powers, to be viewed in those invaluable lessons of religion, love of country, and morality; such subjects are worthy of being placed in view as the most instructive records to a rising generation.*

Rembrandt Peale was impressed with the grand historical subjects and came to believe that such was the direction his own career should take. He returned to Philadelphia in 1803 resolved to paint no more portraits.

Unfortunately, response to Peale's large historical scenes was lukewarm. He spent some time in France around 1809, where he experimented with encaustic, a waxy medium that, though excellent for enriching coloration, was less useful for the subtle delineation that Peale used to create character in his subjects. In 1814 he moved to Baltimore to try his luck there but met with little success. By 1822 he was again painting portraits in Philadelphia.

Cheekwood's *Portrait of a Man* portrays the characteristics that are typical of Rembrandt Peale's portraits after 1810: large, deep-set eyes, a full mouth, and puffy facial features. The wider countenance and manipulation of light and shadow, utilized with many of Peale's male subjects, allowed the artist to create a penetrating sense of character. The portrait's depth of expression suggests that it was painted during Peale's mature period, between 1810 and 1830. His later works are less psychologically expressive. It was during those twenty years that the artist spent most of his time painting images of George Washington, which allowed him to delve into history and yet produce a marketable product.

Portrait of a Man, N.D., OIL ON CANVAS, GIFT OF MR. AND MRS. WALTER KNESTRICK, 1986.16.18

Cheat River Gorge, N.D., OIL ON CANVAS, GIFT OF MR. AND MRS. FRED F. LUCAS, 1972.6.11

ARTIST UNKNOWN, AMERICAN, HUDSON RIVER SCHOOL

In subject, size, and style, this depiction of the Cheat River Gorge in Coopers Rock State Forest, West Virginia, painted by an unknown artist, typifies the Hudson River School. Fascinated by the grandeur of nature, the proponents of this first American school created ethereal scenes of the American wilderness, infused with the glimmering light that they associated with the divine. The monumental perspective of the deep gorge and distant, hazily blue mountains dwarf the three figures gazing west toward the river below. The insignificance of man in the face of holy nature seems apparent, too, in the large size of the painting, as if the subject is too important to be contained within the dimensions of the standard-size canvas.

Centered in the foreground of the painting, between the branches of the Cheat River, appears a dying tree, juxtaposed to a young sapling. This allusion to the cycle of life, common to Hudson River School landscapes, symbolizes the new emerging from the old, whether young Americans grafted from old European roots, a reborn country surviving the deadly Civil War, or a new forest growing out of an area ravaged by America's westward migration. That movement west is also symbolized in the railroad trestle entering the picture from the lower right. More than any other technological development, the railroads would change the face of America by moving the population west to the Pacific Ocean. Here they function as the very symbol of Manifest Destiny, the nineteenth-century assertion that westward expansion was America's sacred responsibility.

Formally, the scene is a series of converging angled lines, all leading to the center of the painting. The viewer is led into the painting by means of natural and man-made diagonals: the sunlight, the river, and the railroad. All are arranged to suggest a divine order in nature. The tree, as the only strong vertical element of the painting, commands the viewer's attention. The small foreground figures, which are only dabs of blue, red, and yellow paint, appear insignificant in the natural surroundings. They are dependent on nature, not the other way around. They speak to the human need for the wilderness, as espoused in Henry David Thoreau's *Walden, or Life in the Woods* (1854): "I went to the woods because I wished to live deliberately, to front only the essential facts of life, and see if I could not learn what it had to teach, and not, when I came to die, discover that I had not lived."

WILLIAM MASON BROWN (AMERICAN, 1828–1899), *Landscape with Two Indians,* N.D., OIL ON CANVAS, TRANSFER FROM THE NASHVILLE MUSEUM OF ART, GIFT OF DR. AND MRS. GEORGE W. HALE, 1960.2.17 THE ENORMITY OF BROWN'S AMERICAN WILDERNESS DWARFS HIS DEPICTION OF NATIVE AMERICANS.

KENNETH RILEY (AMERICAN, B. 1919), *Aravaipa,* N.D., ACRYLIC ON MASONITE, GIFT OF MR. AND MRS. JOHN A. HILL, 1991.10.35 ARTISTS WORKING IN THE AMERICAN SOUTHWEST SHARED A COMMON INTEREST IN DEPICTING THE LAND.

SVEN SVENSON (AMERICAN, B. NORWAY, 1864–1930), *Winter Landscape,* 1896, OIL ON CANVAS, GIFT OF MR. AND MRS. JAMES AVENT, 1981.16.1

PHOTOGRAPH OF WILLIAM BRADFORD c. 1885. EMMA WOOTON DeLONG PAPERS, 1928-1950. ARCHIVES OF AMERICAN ART. SMITHSONIAN INSTITUTION.

WILLIAM BRADFORD (AMERICAN, 1823–1892)

Landscape painters of the mid-nineteenth century categorized their subjects by three terms: the beautiful, the picturesque, and the sublime. Beautiful landscapes, according to Sue Rainey in *Creating Picturesque America*, were typically calm, idealized scenes. The picturesque was characterized by contrast and irregularity, created to provoke curiosity in the viewer. Sublime landscapes were awe-inspiring, dramatic scenes of mountain peaks, raging rivers, and impressive canyons. William Bradford was part of a generation of mid-nineteenth-century American painters who found evidence of the divine in the country's sublime landscape. Today, we call these painters the Hudson River School because the art movement developed in the northeastern region and emphasized the mountains and vistas of the Hudson River Valley. A small number of marine painters, including Bradford, are also associated with the school because of their dramatic arctic scenes.

It became common in the nineteenth century for artists to accompany explorers on polar expeditions. Over time, the incredible scenery and public demand led artists to undertake their own expeditions. But whereas northern subjects were interspersed in the works of artists such as Frederic Church and James Hamilton, William Bradford devoted his career to painting, writing, and lecturing exclusively about the arctic.

Bradford studied painting with the Dutch artist Albert van Beest (1820–1860) in Fairhaven, Massachusetts, in 1853. Van Beest trained Bradford to create realistic, detailed marine scenes, which Bradford sold for $25.00. Encouraged by his success, Bradford departed for Labrador later that year, the first in a series of arctic trips that he would make in the 1860s. He returned from these voyages with sketches and photographs that he would use for paintings over the next twenty years. From a logbook from his 1865 journey, he published his highly successful *Arctic Regions* in 1873, which includes this account:

> *The scene was wild, strange, and magnificent; a summer's sun in the distance shone out with the steady gleam of frosted silver. Not a breath of wind was stirring, and the deep blue of an arctic sky was reflected in the water so strangely flecked with indescribable icy forms, from dead white to glossy, glistening satin; from the deepest green to all the lightest shades; and from faint blue to deepest "lapis lazuli"; and again, as some lofty berg passed between us and the sun, its crest would be bordered with an orange-coloured halo.*

Bradford received two important accolades in the early 1870s: a commission by Queen Victoria for a painting that was exhibited in the Royal Academy of Arts in London, and membership in the prestigious National Academy of Design. Some have suggested that his work from the 1870s and 1880s lost some of the detailed realism of his earlier work, possibly due to the boredom that accompanies overproduction. Bradford may also have been responding to the looser, less-precise style of the French Impressionists that had begun to take hold in the American art market. He spent most of the last decade of his life lecturing about the arctic region.

Sunset in the Arctic, N.D., OIL ON CANVAS, GIFT OF MR. HANS ANDERSEN, 1998.11.3

Entrance to the Harbor — Breezy Morning, 1869, OIL ON CANVAS, GIFT OF MR. HANS ANDERSEN, 1998.11.10

JAMES HAMILTON (AMERICAN, 1819–1878)

James Hamilton was the son of an Irish cordwainer, or shoemaker, who immigrated to this country in the mid-1830s. Hamilton showed a talent for drawing at an early age and found a patron in Philadelphia to pay for art classes. Over time, though, his distinctive technique developed more from emulating other artists. John Sartain, a Philadelphia engraver, was a primary source of advice and support for the young Hamilton, but it was Hamilton's exposure to the painting of J. M. W. Turner that changed the way he worked.

America's art schools took root in the first half of the nineteenth century. The Pennsylvania Academy of the Fine Arts, the first American school of art, had been established in 1805, making Philadelphia one of the best locations for a young artist. The National Academy of Design in New York City followed suit in 1826. Hamilton exhibited at both schools (Pennsylvania in 1843, New York in 1846), but we have no evidence that he took any classes at the academies. Like so many artists of the period, including Gilbert Stuart, Thomas Sully, and Samuel F. B. Morse, Hamilton traveled to England to study the work of European painters.

By 1864, the time of his departure for England, Hamilton had established himself in Philadelphia as a painter of prominence. His first big break had occurred in 1843 when his *Scene on the Delaware* received favorable notice at a Pennsylvania Academy exhibition. By 1849 his paintings were selling out at such shows.

The trip to Europe proved to be a watershed for Hamilton, who adopted the loose brush and romantic character of Turner's paintings. In *Entrance to the Harbor* the influence of Turner is marked in the romantic light cast by the descending sun near the center of the canvas and by the loose, expressive brush stroke. Americans showed mixed response to Hamilton's new work. Although some called him "the American Turner," others complained that Hamilton's quick brush left out the details of his subjects.

Hamilton continued to paint romantic marine scenes of the mid-Atlantic for the next twenty years. He also illustrated books. By the 1870s his popularity with the art-buying public diminished, perhaps because Hamilton oversupplied the market with too many paintings of similar subject and style. At the same time, interest in American painting was being supplanted by renewed enthusiasm for European subjects, which would dominate the market until after World War II. In the late 1870s Hamilton sold over one hundred of his paintings to finance a final journey around the world. He made it to San Francisco, where he died before completing the trip.

COMPARISONS:

JAMES HAMILTON (AMERICAN, 1819–1878), *Ships Along the Coast,* N.D., WATERCOLOR, GIFT OF MR. HANS ANDERSEN, 1998.11.11

JAMES HAMILTON (AMERICAN, 1819–1878), *The Old Navy Yard,* N.D., PENCIL, GIFT OF MR. HANS ANDERSEN, 1998.11.12
THE NAVY'S SHIPS WERE BUILT AND REPAIRED IN THE NAVY YARDS, WHICH ARE LOCATED IN NUMEROUS PORTS, INCLUDING HAMILTON'S HOMETOWN, PHILADELPHIA.

PHOTOGRAPH OF JAMES HAMILTON, 1866. PHOTOGRAPHED BY GEORGE W. CONNARROE. THE PENNSYLVANIA ACADEMY OF THE FINE ARTS, PHILADELPHIA. GIFT OF JOHN FREDERICK LEWIS.

THOMAS WATERMAN WOOD (AMERICAN, 1823–1903), *The Sapphire Slipper*, N.D., OIL ON CANVAS, MUSEUM PURCHASE THROUGH THE BEQUEST OF ANITA BEVILL MCMICHAEL STALLWORTH, 1989.2 THE DISHEVELED APPEARANCE OF THE GIRL HOLDING HER SHOE SUGGESTS THAT THE PORTRAIT WAS PAINTED AFTER HER DEATH, REFLECTING A TRADITIONAL BELIEF THAT CHILDREN LOST TO DEATH BEYOND THEIR PARENTS' REACH BECOME UNKEMPT. SHE POINTS TO A GROUP OF BUILDINGS ACROSS A RIVER, POSSIBLY A REPRESENTATION OF EARLY NASHVILLE.

JACOB LAWRENCE (AMERICAN, 1917–2000), *The 1920's — The Migrants Cast Their Ballots,* 1974, SILKSCREEN, ED. 92/125, GIFT OF THE LORILLARD COMPANY, 1976.4.30

PHOTOGRAPH OF THOMAS WATERMAN WOOD, COURTESY OF THE THOMAS WATERMAN WOOD ART GALLERY, MONTPELIER, VERMONT

THOMAS WATERMAN WOOD (AMERICAN, 1823–1903)

His First Vote is actually a detail of a larger painting, *American Citizens* (*To the Polls*), that Thomas Waterman Wood painted in 1867. The subtitle of the larger painting appears in the sign above the voter's head. The figure in *His First Vote* is one of four in the larger painting: a Northerner (Yankee), an Irishman, a Dutchman, and the African American pictured here. The model for *His First Vote* was probably the same man Wood had employed in a previous three-painting series called *War Episodes* (1866),* when he was a resident of Louisville. Waiting in line with the other voters, who smoke, whittle, or fidget, the African American is the only one of the four who appears to be focused on his task. This is hardly surprising, since African Americans had just gained citizenship through the Fourteenth Amendment to the Constitution, ratified in 1868. The first legal vote by an African American actually took place in 1867 in New Orleans, making this a timely scene. Nevertheless, full voting rights for former slaves would not be confirmed until 1870 in the Fifteenth Amendment.

At the time *His First Vote* was painted, the artist had only recently moved to New York City, having resided in Louisville from 1862 to the fall of 1866 and, before that, in Nashville for three years. Before that, Wood had worked as an itinerant portrait painter along the East coast for several years before spending a year in Europe. Even while in New York, Wood took his summers in his hometown of Montpelier, Vermont, where he drew many of the character studies incorporated in his later paintings. Unlike many artists of the period, Wood did not caricature his African American subjects. He captured a sense of the rural life that was quickly disappearing with post–Civil War industrialization. Genre subjects (scenes from everyday life) such as *His First Vote* were Wood's bread and butter. Because their moral messages upheld the middle class Puritan work ethic, they were well received by the public.

In 1874 Wood took up residence in New York's famous Tenth Street Studio, a building housing other successful genre artists, including John George Brown (1831–1913) and Seymour Guy (1824–1910). Their sentimental brand of genre painting enchanted Victorian America in search of moral values. By 1880 Thomas Waterman Wood had also fallen under its spell. With few exceptions, Wood's later works express a sentimental character that fails to match the quality exhibited in such earlier paintings as *His First Vote*. Wood's popularity evaporated soon after his death in 1903, as America's taste for European Impressionism grew. Renewed interest in Thomas Waterman Wood recently resurfaced in the 1970s, when the country's bicentennial renewed interest in early American genre.

*War Episodes WAS EXHIBITED AT THE NATIONAL ACADEMY OF DESIGN IN 1869, WHERE IT WON WOOD THE LEVEL OF ASSOCIATE IN THE ACADEMY. WOOD BECAME A FULL ACADEMICIAN IN 1871.

His First Vote, 1868, OIL ON BOARD, MUSEUM PURCHASE THROUGH THE BEQUEST of ANITA BEVILL McMICHAEL STALLWORTH, 1991.2.2

The Whistling Boy, 1872, OIL ON CANVAS, GIFT OF MRS. HUGH STALLWORTH, 1976.6.42

FRANK DUVENECK (AMERICAN, 1849–1919)

Frank Duveneck created this sketch of *The Whistling Boy* as a study for his renowned, full-length painting of the same title and year. The style of this piece, as with the majority of Duveneck's work, is what Norbert Heermann, his former student, described in 1918 as "simple and direct . . . without technical tricks for effect, without persuasive story subjects, without even so much self-consciousness as is implied in the word 'sentiment.'" It was Duveneck's honest, confident handling of paint, as well as his universal openness to life and the subjects it provided, that sparked his meteoric rise at the Munich Royal Academy from 1870–1873.

Duveneck's paintings during this period exhibit the influence of Munich Royal Academy teacher Wilhelm von Diez and of Diez's great enthusiasm for Europe's Old Masters of the seventeenth century—artists such as Frans Hals, Diego Rodriguez Velázquez, and Rembrandt. Although the dark tonalities and golden hues of the Old Master paintings were often the result of yellowed varnish and grime, Diez, as well as Duveneck and his peers, associated these somber colors with the intentions of the artists they strove to emulate. The resulting body of student work, especially that of the early 1870s, could be characterized as virtually monochromatic and filled with hues of sienna, black, and umber. The Munich artists who painted in this style during the 1870s and 1880s eventually became known as the Munich School.

From the boy's jagged hairline to the unraveling imagery at the canvas's bottom edge, this sketch for *Whistling Boy* is a superb example of Duveneck's greatest artistic strength—his brushwork. Duveneck's ability to paint with loose brush strokes while maintaining scrupulous control of the paint's application marked him as a rising young star of the Munich School and prompted art historian Robert Neuhaus to write, "The almost magical manipulative power Frank Duveneck possessed with his loaded brush constituted the most exciting and distinguishing quality of his canvases."

Although Duveneck's brushwork remained a distinctive mark of his paintings, his color palette and subject matter began to change in the late 1870s. Influenced by the geography, architecture, and art of Italy during his frequent visits to Venice and Florence, Duveneck developed an interest in outdoor or plein air painting. During his development of a lighter, more impressionistic style, Duveneck began to abandon the dark, umber palette of the Munich School that had so heavily influenced him as a young artist.

Just as Duveneck's technique evolved throughout the years, so did his selection of subjects, which ranged from street urchins to female nudes to sailboats at Gloucester. It was his realistic, street-life paintings like *Whistling Boy*, however, that inspired a new generation of American painters to adopt similarly gritty subjects. The Ashcan School, which included Robert Henri, George Luks, Everett Shinn, and John Sloan, represents the clearest distillation of Duveneck's influence. Using loose brush strokes and hurried renderings of working-class people and settings, those painters, many having worked as newspaper illustrators, paid homage to artists such as Duveneck, who cleared the way for their brand of urban realism in the fine arts.

COMPARISON:

W. EUGENE SMITH (AMERICAN, 1918–1978) *Boys Picking*, N.D., FROM *the Migrant Workers Essay*, GELATIN SILVER PRINT, GIFT OF MR. JAY RUDBERG, 1985.17.1.5

PHOTOGRAPH OF FRANK DUVENECK, ARCHIVES OF AMERICAN ART. SMITHSONIAN INSTITUTION.

COMPARISON:

ROBERT HENRI (AMERICAN, 1865–1929),
Slender Trees and Green Leaves,
N.D., PASTEL ON PAPER, GIFT OF
MR. AND MRS. WALTER KNESTRICK, 1981.26.7

PHOTOGRAPH OF GEORGE INNESS, C. 1890.
PHOTOGRAPHED BY E. S. BENNETT. PHOTOGRAPHS OF
ARTISTS COLLECTION I. ARCHIVES OF AMERICAN ART.
SMITHSONIAN INSTITUTION.

GEORGE INNESS (AMERICAN, 1825–1894)

In George Inness's sketch *Milton on the Hudson*, the artist portrays man and nature as being in perfect harmony. The painting's silhouettes—which merge into tree trunks, recline on the overgrown forest floor, and stand under the veil of a tree's shadow—have little identity of their own. Even the two figures allowed to stand separated from rooted growth turn to each other beneath the black shadow of an ancient tree. This visual unity of man and nature in *Milton on the Hudson* is reminiscent of the Eastern philosophy of "mutual arising," the belief that, although distinct from each other, one's inside arises mutually with the outside, making the two inseparable. This is not coincidental, as Inness was influenced by the similar teachings of Western theosophist Emanuel Swendenborg, who believed that god, nature, and man are inextricably linked.

Milton on the Hudson is also Inness's testimony to the transcendent function of landscape in art and life. The serene postures of the figures and the effulgent, yellow light framed by symmetrical trees make little reference to the destructive and chaotic aspects of nature. Inness, like many artists before and since, created a composition that strives to bring harmony and order to a chaotic world. In *Milton on the Hudson* we see the result of Inness's desire to avoid what he described as "thought alone or . . . feeling alone" and to reveal both "will and understanding."

This reverence for nature was especially fashionable during Inness's lifetime, notably in the paintings of the Hudson River School, whose finely detailed work sought to aggrandize the American landscape. Influenced by Swendenborg's philosophy, Inness abandoned the approach of the Hudson River painters and journeyed to France in 1854, where he studied the landscapes of the Barbizon School, the first group to emphasize painting out of doors. Inness's quest to transcend the mere rendering of sublime grandiosity in the landscape and to portray nature as an invaluable, mystical link between man and his creator led him to create poetic and painterly works like *Milton on the Hudson.*

Inness has been quoted as saying, "You must suggest to me reality, you can never show me reality." This philosophy of intimate response to the land, although adhered to by Inness for twenty years prior, became popular among the majority of American landscape painters in the late 1870s. Inness's belief that "the true use of art is, first, to cultivate the artist's own spiritual nature, and secondly, to enter as a factor in general civilization" can now be heard as the anthem of a modern thinker ahead of his time.

By the late 1800s, Inness's style became more accepted. Magazines such as *the Century* praised him in 1877 as "one of our older artists who has not fallen into the ruts either of ignorance or indifference. . . . The artist has lost none of the force, and what is still more remarkable, none of the curiosity of youth." By the 1870s, the artistic generation of the Hudson River School was being viewed as provincial, while Inness had become a vital influence to a retinue of aspiring artists.

Milton on the Hudson, (SKETCH), C. 1882, OIL ON LINEN, GIFT OF MR. AND MRS. WALTER KNESTRICK, 1981.26.8

Who Wins May Wear, 1882, oil on canvas, Gift of Mr. and Mrs. Peter DaPuzzo, 1995.14

LEMUEL WILMARTH (AMERICAN, 1835–1918)

In his poem, the British poet Edmund Waller (1606–1687) alludes to the story of the Greek god of music, poetry, and medicine, Phoebus Apollo, who loved the nymph Daphne. In the myth Daphne rejects her suitor and is changed into a bay or laurel tree by her father, the river god Peneus. Apollo honors his lost love by vowing to wear a wreath of bay leaves as a crown. The bay or laurel wreath became a symbol of triumph worn by victors at the Pythic games held every eight years at Delphi, Apollo's home. Other Panhellenic festivals rewarded their athletes with wreathes of different leaves: olive at Olympia, pine at Isthmia, and parsley at Nemea. Because Delphi's laurel leaf is evergreen, it also attaches an immortal quality to the athlete's achievements. While in Paris, Wilmarth would have seen images of laurel wreaths on the Greek vases in the Louvre, where he studied with the artist Leon Gerome prior to 1867.

As Waller refers to the poet's public successes, so Lemuel Wilmarth refers to victory in his painting, in which the centrally placed figure twines a laurel wreath. Such neoclassical elements were endorsed by the National Academy of Design, the country's leading art school during the last half of the nineteenth century. The Academy promoted myth, history, and religion as the only appropriate subjects for fine art. Wilmarth, the first instructor of the Academy and an academician himself, was aware of the Academy's preferences; *Who Wins May Wear* was selected and exhibited there in 1882.

Yet what he sang in his immortal strain,
Though unsuccessful, was not sung in vain.
All but the nymph that should redress his wrong,
Attend his passion and approve his song.
Like Phoebus thus, acquiring unsought praise,
He caught at love and filled his arms with bays.

—EDMUND WALLER, "THE STORY OF PHOEBUS AND DAPHNE, APPLIED"

Other neoclassical references in the painting include the chair covered with an oriental carpet and the tasseled drapery to the sitter's left. These decorative elements were frequently employed in paintings of the period by Wilmarth's peers at the Tenth Street Studio, the first building dedicated solely to art studios and exhibitions. From 1871 to 1890 Wilmarth lived and worked at the Tenth Street Studio, where the forty-nine residents enjoyed great camaraderie and interaction. The individual studios were renowned for their eccentric collections of rare and unusual objects, used by the artists in their portraits and genre scenes. This was particularly true in the case of Wilmarth's friend William Merritt Chase, who produced a series of paintings of his highly decorated Tenth Street studio between 1880 and 1885.

Lemuel Wilmarth's neoclassical style was falling from fashion by 1890. Wilmarth himself had organized the Art Students League in 1875, a group that promoted artistic freedom in the choosing of subjects. Nevertheless, he tried unsuccessfully to reconcile the League's position with that of the conservative Academy. Public interest in Wilmarth's sugary-sweet subjects declined, and references to his work in American art journals ceased until the 1970s, which saw a resurgence of interest in the neoclassical.

EMILE-ANTOINE BOURDELLE (FRENCH, 1861–1929), *Penelope,* 1909, BRONZE, GIFT OF MRS. WALTER SHARP, 1983.5.1 BOURDELLE'S STATUE OF ODYSSEUS'S WIFE, PENELOPE, TESTIFIES TO ARTISTS' TIMELESS FASCINATION WITH THE POWER OF MYTH.

ARTHUR B. DAVIES, *Two Figures in a Landscape,* 1910, OIL ON CANVAS, GIFT OF MR. THOMAS LEWYN, 1982.15.11.5 DAVIES' PAINTING SUGGESTS ANOTHER BIBLICAL THEME, THAT OF THE EXPULSION FROM THE GARDEN OF EDEN.

ARTHUR B. DAVIES (AMERICAN, 1862–1928), *Idyllic Landscape,* c. 1912, OIL ON CANVAS, GIFT OF THE 1996 AND 1997 COLLECTORS' GROUPS WITH MATCHING FUNDS THROUGH THE BEQUEST OF ANITA BEVILL MCMICHAEL STALLWORTH, 1997.3.3 THE FIGURES IN DAVIES' LATER PAINTINGS ARE RARELY PORTRAITS OF INDIVIDUALS BUT, INSTEAD, ARE SYLVAN CREATURES PLACED IN BUCOLIC SETTINGS.

PHOTOGRAPH OF ARTHUR B. DAVIES. PHOTOGRAPHED BY PETER A. JULEY & SON. PHOTOGRAPHS OF ARTISTS COLLECTION I. ARCHIVES OF AMERICAN ART. SMITHSONIAN INSTITUTION.

ARTHUR B. DAVIES (AMERICAN, 1862–1928)

O tender yearning, sweet hoping!
The golden time of first love!
The eye sees the open heaven,
The heart is intoxicated with bliss;
O that the beautiful time of young love
Could remain green forever.
—*John Christoph Friedrich von Schiller,*
"THE SONG OF THE BELL," 1799

In 1891 Arthur B. Davies was courting physician Virginia Merriweather in her hometown of Congers, New York, where farmland meets the Hudson River. Davies, then twenty-nine, painted his young lover in this bucolic setting including spring lilacs blossoming in the background. Daisies* adorn her long brown hair as she carries a bouquet of what appear to be rose buds in her left hand. As the son of British immigrants, Davies would have participated in May Day festivities, which celebrated Flora, the Greek goddess of spring, with May poles decorated in garlands of flowers. The theme was well known to artists throughout history. Rembrandt van Rijin painted his second wife, Saskia, three times as Flora. Botticelli's well-known *Allegory of Spring* (c. 1481), a wedding gift, we believe, for Lorenzo d'Medici's cousin, also depicts Flora, as well as her lover, Zephyrus, the god of the west wind. Davies' portrayal of Virginia Merriweather includes blustery winds that suggest the approach of Zephyrus.

The doves hovering above Virginia's head are well known as Christian symbols of the divine spirit. Descending from the heavens, doves are also used to portray love, as in the luxurious passages of the "Song of Solomon" that refer to the turtledove when the shepherd entreats his love to come away with him. Davies, whose father was a Methodist minister, would likely have been familiar with the Biblical love song. Turtle doves—an Old World genus with a long, graduated tail—are often used as symbols of eternal love because they mate for life.

Davies was fascinated by symbolism, which became increasingly important in his later work. He would have known Symbolist illustration from *Harper's Bazaar* and *Scribners* magazine, and from *Century Magazine,* where Davies himself worked as an illustrator. Davies argued for the inclusion of European Symbolists in the important Armory Show of 1913, which introduced a great number of American artists to the avant-garde.

The flowers appear on the earth;
the time of singing has come,
and the voice of the turtledove
is heard in our land.
—"SONG OF SOLOMON," 2:13

Davies and Merriweather were married the year after this painting was completed and moved to Congers, where Arthur tried his hand at farm work. Regretfully, Davies' loving relationship with his wife did not last. Two sons were born, but the marriage proved to be troubled, and Arthur moved back to New York City by 1900. Arthur and Virginia remained married to each other for the rest of their lives, but in name only.

*DAISIES WERE ORIGINALLY CALLED "DAY'S EYES" BECAUSE OF THEIR YELLOW CENTERS AND BECAUSE THEY CLOSE THEIR PETALS AT DUSK AND OPEN THEM TO MEET THE MORNING SUN.

Girl with Doves, 1891, OIL ON CANVAS, GIFT OF THE 1994 SWAN BALL
PATRONS WITH MATCHING FUNDS THROUGH THE BEQUEST OF ANITA BEVILL
MCMICHAEL STALLWORTH, 1994.6

Portrait of the Schiff Children, 1892, OIL ON CANVAS, TRANSFER FROM THE NASHVILLE MUSEUM OF ART, GIFT OF MR. CHARLES SCHIFF BURCH, 1960.2.68

JULIAN STORY (AMERICAN, B. ENGLAND, 1857–1916)

Julian Story was born in England in 1857, the son of expatriate poet and sculptor William Westmore Story. While in Europe he was a pupil of Frank Duveneck, Gustave Boulanger, and Jules Lefebvre. Early in his career, Story worked in the romantic figurative genre, but by 1887 his main subject was portraiture. Most of his later work is in the manner of the fashionable portraitists of the day, such as John Singer Sargent and James McNeil Whistler. Upon his arrival in the United States, Story was elected an associate of the National Academy of Design and taught at the Pennsylvania Academy of the Fine Arts.

These are the children of Mr. and Mrs. Charles Theophilus Schiff. In 1891 the family moved from Ohio to England, where Story did this portrait a year later. The family included seven children, five of which are shown here dressed in fashionable attire for the time (from left to right): Martin, Catherine, Mary, Charles, and Lucille. White clothing has long symbolized purity, especially for children. Young girls from wealthy Victorian families wore smocked dresses and aprons in pastel colors, distinguishing them and their family from the working classes. Young Edward VII's love of naval regalia inspired the popularity of sailor suits for young boys.

The Asian-inspired interior of the Schiff's London home was a common motif in aristocratic Victorian homes. The exhibition of the collection of artifacts belonging to Rutherford Alcock, the first British consul general to Japan, at the London International Exposition of 1892 reflected the popularity of style in England. Many homes contained entire rooms devoted to the trend, the best known of which is the Peacock Room painted by James McNeil Whistler for the London dining room of F. R. Leyland. The Schiff's small Japanese table and Persian carpets were typical accessories for such rooms.

While the painting's background is important to the composition, it is the vivid pillows that draw focus to the children. They are presented in casual poses, interacting with each other and the viewer. Because of their relative rarity and expense in colder climates, citrus fruits, like the orange Martin offers his siblings, were used as a symbol of wealth. A vase of lilies not only adds balance to the right side of the composition, but also symbolizes purity and calls attention to the Aesthetic movement that influenced Story.

ALICE SCHILLE (AMERICAN, 1869–1955), *Easter Sunday,* 1930, OIL ON CANVAS, GIFT OF *THE NASHVILLE BANNER,* 1988.15

WASHINGTON BOGART COOPER (AMERICAN, 1802–1840), *The Thomas Foster Family,* c. 1850, OIL ON CANVAS, GIFT OF MRS. JERRY C. BURNS, 1986.11

WILLIAM MERRITT CHASE (AMERICAN, 1849-1916), *Portrait of Mrs. N. Lansing Zabriskie,* 1894, OIL ON CANVAS, GIFT OF MR. AND MRS. WALTER KNESTRICK, 1981.26.3 THIS PORTRAIT EXEMPLIFIES THE POWERFUL, FLUID BRUSH STROKE FOR WHICH CHASE WAS KNOWN.

WILLIAM MERRITT CHASE (AMERICAN, 1849-1916), *The Smoker — Portrait of Frank Duveneck,* 1875, ETCHING, MUSEUM PURCHASE THROUGH THE BEQUEST OF ANITA BEVILL MCMICHAEL STALLWORTH, 1993.1 CHASE AND ARTIST FRANK DUVENECK WERE BOTH STUDENTS AT THE ROYAL ACADEMY IN MUNICH DURING THE EARLY 1870s AND SPENT MUCH TIME PAINTING, TRAVELING, AND STUDYING TOGETHER. THIS PORTRAIT, WHICH CHASE PAINTED IN OIL IN 1876, REFLECTS BOTH ARTISTS' INTERESTS IN OLD MASTER PAINTINGS.

PHOTOGRAPH OF WILLIAM MERRITT CHASE. PHOTOGRAPHED BY HAESELER. PHOTOGRAPHS OF ARTISTS COLLECTION I. ARCHIVES OF AMERICAN ART. SMITHSONIAN INSTITUTION

After great success infusing Impressionism into the American art scene, William Merritt Chase often returned to an "Old Masters" style of painting. As seen in *Dorothy in Black,* Chase did not use the bright, colorful palette and wispy brush strokes for which his work of the 1880s was known. Instead, he reverted back to his early training in Munich, using darker, duller colors spread thickly and broadly. In this painting, Dorothy's shape appears flat, reminiscent of Japanese prints. Likewise, she holds a fan in her lap, suggesting the upper class's new fascination with Asian art and artifacts. Dressed simply in a black dress, Dorothy appears austere, confrontational, and somber.

During the late nineteenth and early twentieth centuries, American arts continued to struggle for legitimacy in the dominating presence of European art. American painters were viewed as "second class" artists when compared to innovative European art circles. Many nineteenth century American artists, such as John Singer Sargent and James Abbott McNeil Whistler, relocated to Europe to pursue critical or commercial acclaim. To Americans, most artists appeared eccentric, bohemian, and outside the realm of society. Chase and his comrades in the Tenth Street Studio group made a conscious effort to change how Americans viewed American artists. Chase convinced some artists to alter their appearance by dressing in business suits, to present themselves as professionals. Many artists, roused by Chase's extravagant studio, lavishly decorated their ateliers with exotic foreign collectibles and lush fabrics. The atmosphere of the studio lent a mystique to these artists along with an air of wisdom and upper-class sensibility. Artists who followed this formula were soon perceived as intellectuals as well as a businessmen.

William Merritt Chase not only raised the status of artists but that of art teachers as well, becoming one of the most renowned art instructors in the late nineteenth and early twentieth centuries. Unlike his contemporaries who considered teaching a lowly and time-consuming occupation, Chase found extraordinary satisfaction in contributing his knowledge and ideas to future generations of artists. Throughout his career, he fought academic notions of painting in the hope that students would rely on their own creativity and not be entirely bound by rules and formulas. He encouraged respect for techniques learned in school and for the study of Old Master paintings, but he urged study of contemporary artists as well and the development of individualistic styles. Chase stressed the importance of stylistic experimentation with subjects that inspired artists' imaginations. Ironically, as modernist movements swept over Europe and penetrated the minds of American artists, Chase sharply criticized his students who followed avant-garde theories. Among many of Chase's famous students who broke from his now conservative ideals were Georgia O'Keeffe and Joseph Stella.

Dorothy in Black, c. 1892, oil on canvas, Museum Purchase through the Fine Art Acquisition Fund in memory of Mr. David Steine with contributions from Mr. and Mrs. George Clark, Exchange Club Charities, Mr. and Mrs. Jack Massey, Mr. and Mrs. John Stamps, and Mr. and Mrs. Albert Werthan, 1976.10.6

Winter Landscape, 1897, oil on canvas, Gift of Mr. and Mrs. Ervin Entrekin, 1981.2.7

JULIAN ALDEN WEIR (AMERICAN, 1852–1919)

From childhood, Julian Alden Weir was surrounded by art and nature. His father, Robert W. Weir (1803–1889), worked as a landscape drawing instructor at Westpoint Military Academy for forty years. His brother, John Ferguson Weir (1841–1926), went on to teach at Yale's School of Fine Arts from 1869 to 1913. Robert Weir would spend hours with the boys in his Hudson River studio, examining maps and prints and talking about the land and the lives of the great artists. Robert's lasting gifts to his son were a respect for the skill of drawing and an admiration of nature. In a letter to his brother in 1875, J. Alden wrote,

I will throw my whims to the dogs when I get back to Paris and dig in at the schools, as a simple representer of nature, searching for the character and individuality of the thing that is before me. . . .

After his marriage to Anna Baker, Weir divided his time between their New York residence, the Baker home in Windham, Connecticut, and his farm in Branchville, a small agricultural Connecticut community near Bridgeport. Situated between the artist colonies of Old Lyme and Cos Cob, Branchville was an ideal location for Weir. He could teach at Cos Cob in the winter (as he did with John Twachtman in 1892 and 1893) and at the Art Students League in the summer (the train to Manhattan took under an hour). It was in Branchville that Weir created a series of snowscapes, beginning in 1894 and culminating with paintings like *Winter Landscape* in 1897.

The painting's high horizon and truncated trees create a horizontality that owes much to the flattened perspective of Japanese prints. Japanese artwork became popular in America at the end of the nineteenth century, in large part due to its introduction at the London International Exposition of 1892. Furthermore, we know from Theodore Robinson's diary that Weir was studying Japanese prints in 1893 and 1894.

In the year that *Winter Landscape* was painted, Weir helped to found the "Ten," a group of American Impressionists who resigned in protest from the Society of American Artists in December of 1897. The group–Weir, John Twachtman, Childe Hassam, Willard Metcalf, Thomas Dewing, Edmund Tarbell, Frank Benson, Joseph de Camp, Robert Reid, and Edward Simmons–wanted to hold small exhibits of Impressionistic works, whereas the Society's large exhibits were dominated by Barbizon paintings. Although Weir is associated with the Ten, he was never an Impressionist in the full sense of the word. His initial response to the new style, which he first encountered in Paris in 1877, was unfavorable, made clear in this letter to his parents, undoubtedly because of his reverence for careful drawing that his father had instilled in him:

I went across the river the other day to see an exhibition of the work of a new school which call themselves "Impressionists." I never in my life saw more horrible things.

Later, Weir adopted some of the style's tenets, as his brush stroke loosened and his palette lightened. He had always preferred to paint outdoors (what the Impressionists called plein air painting), but Weir did not seek to explore atmosphere as a heightened sensory experience. More importantly, Weir's subjects, like this painting's tree root ball, have a sense of tangible weight not found in the French Impressionists, who treated objects and the space between them equally across the canvas.

COMPARISONS:

FRANK WESTON BENSON (AMERICAN, 1862–1951), *Lady in White*, N.D., OIL ON CANVAS, GIFT OF MR. AND MRS. WALTER KNESTRICK, 1986.16.5
A MEMBER OF THE TEN, BENSON WAS A CLOSE FRIEND OF WEIR'S, SPENDING SUMMERS AT WEIR'S BRANCHVILLE HOME. BENSON, EDMUND TARBELL, AND ROBERT REID ATTENDED WEIR'S MARRIAGE TO ELLA BAKER IN 1893, WHERE JOHN HENRY TWACHTMAN SERVED AS BEST MAN.

WOLF KAHN (AMERICAN, B. 1927), *Copse*, 1979–1980, OIL ON CANVAS, MUSEUM PURCHASE THROUGH THE WERTHAN ACQUISITION FUND, 1982.1
KAHN'S CONTEMPORARY NEW ENGLAND LANDSCAPE CONTAINS THE SAME HIGH HORIZON AND QUIET MOOD FOUND IN WEIR'S WINTER SCENE.

PHOTOGRAPH OF JULIAN ALDEN WEIR, c. 1910. PHOTOGRAPHED BY PETER A. JULEY & SON. ARCHIVES OF AMERICAN ART. SMITHSONIAN INSTITUTION.

GEORGE LUKS (AMERICAN, 1867–1933), *Street Scene,* N.D., WATERCOLOR, PENCIL AND WASH ON PAPER BOARD, MUSEUM PURCHASE, 1972.6.12 AS THIS DRAWING SHOWS, LUKS HAD THE ABILITY TO CAPTURE QUICKLY THE ESSENCE OF A STREET SCENE.

GEORGE LUKS (AMERICAN, 1867–1933) *Portrait of Stephen J. Breslin,* 1925, OIL ON CANVAS, GIFT OF MR. AND MRS. WALTER KNESTRICK, 1986.16.17 LUKS'S COMMISSIONED PORTRAITS OFTEN LACK THE SPONTANEITY OF THOSE HE PAINTED FOR HIMSELF.

PHOTOGRAPH OF GEORGE B. LUKS, c. 1908. PHOTOGRAPHED BY PETER A. JULEY & SON. PHOTOGRAPHS OF ARTISTS COLLECTION I. ARCHIVES OF AMERICAN ART. SMITHSONIAN INSTITUTION.

In an era when well-heeled artists ennobled the wealthy through portraiture, George Luks made his reputation painting the homeless, unkempt, impoverished denizens of New York's streets in the early twentieth century. As a young Irish immigrant, Jimmy would have sailed to America with one of the waves of Irish settlers who came to this country following the Great Potato Famine of the mid-nineteenth century. By 1900, New York City had become the home of 3 million Irish immigrants. Ireland, meanwhile, had gone from the most densely populated European country to the least.

The Irish who came to this country could find no work in their homeland. These immigrants had few skills suitable for urban New York and usually settled for the lowest paying and, often, the most dangerous work–duties that skilled workers shunned: cleaning the stables, hauling cargo on the docks, and, after 1900, digging the subway system. Many men died young, leaving boys like Jimmy to care for siblings while their mothers worked in sweatshops or, if they were lucky, as domestics. Jimmy would have lived in one of the Irish enclaves of the city, such as the lower East Side, where overcrowded tenements faced streets smelling of outdoor toilets. For fun, Jimmy likely swam in the sewage-laden East or Harlem Rivers or placed bets at the dog and rat pits. The filth of the streets, the lack of healthy food, and the creeping despair of this lifestyle often led to alcoholism, mental illness, and tuberculosis.

George Luks knew many children like Jimmy. In the late 1890s Luks shared a flat in Greenwich Village with artist William Glackens and frequented Mouquins and other local cafes. Boys like Jimmy would have been a common sight for Luks in these streets. His personal connection to these children enabled Luks to paint his subjects as people who suffer the urban existence of the poor and yet who retain the enthusiasm of youth. Luks played with young Irish immigrants during his boyhood in Williamsport, Pennsylvania. His upper-class family was sympathetic to the Molly Maguires, a group of Irish miners working for better living conditions. The Mollies' widows and children were often in and out of the Luks's household. Luks's immersion in urban life gave him the insight to portray Jimmy not as a subject to be pitied but as a universal expression of childhood. His avoidance of the trap of the maudlin lifts Luks's paintings from the average to the profound.

Jimmy, c. 1908, oil on canvas, Gift of the 1995 Collector's group with matching funds through the bequest of Anita Bevill McMichael Stallworth, 1995.8

Washington Square, c. 1910, oil on canvas, Museum Purchase through the bequest of Anita Bevill McMichael Stallworth, 1995.5

ERNEST LAWSON (AMERICAN, 1873-1939)

At the southern end of Manhattan, Washington Square goes unnoticed by most weekend tourists. As it was during Ernest Lawson's day, the square is the heart of a bohemian district known as Greenwich Village. In 1906 Lawson moved his family from their upper-Manhattan home in Washington Heights to the east side of Washington Square, on MacDougal Alley. The move proved critical for Lawson's career, for there he later met a man who would change his life, the artist William Glackens.

Glackens moved to 29 Washington Square North in 1911. Like Lawson, he was invigorated by the artistic activity in that neighborhood. Originally a swampy area, it served as a potter's field in the early 1800s, complete with a gallows. Washington Square changed dramatically in 1889 when the city commissioned Stanford White to build a monumental arch to celebrate the centennial of George Washington's inauguration. The success of the temporary structure led to a white marble version of the arch, completed in 1892.

But Washington Square was more than a public park: with elegant Fifth Avenue to the north and immigrant tenements to the south, it was the place where social classes met. Bounded by the city's poorer areas, Washington Square attracted urban artists like Glackens and Lawson, as well as Rockwell Kent and Guy Péne du Bois, the socialist John Reed, writers Henry James and Stephen Crane, the patron Gertrude Vanderbilt Whitney, and many other writers and actors who sought inspiration in comfortable surroundings. Glackens and Lawson shared a studio at 64 Washington Square South (now New York University's Loeb Student Center). This scene of Washington Square was painted from that studio sometime between 1906, when Lawson moved to MacDougal Alley, and 1926, when an apartment tower, not in the painting, was built at One Fifth Avenue.

Glackens introduced Lawson to John Sloan, Everett Shinn, and George Luks, all of whom had worked as illustrators in Philadelphia before coming to New York. Together with Robert Henri, Maurice Prendergast, and Arthur B. Davies (the only member of the group not to live in Greenwich Village at some time) Lawson exhibited in 1908 at the MacBeth Gallery, an event that brought public attention to Lawson's work. The group, which came to be known as the Eight, was protesting the National Academy of Design's hanging policies. Lawson's nomination had been rejected by the Academy in 1905; Luks, Glackens, and Shinn were rejected in 1906. The Eight provided a support group for Lawson and the other seven, who often socialized and worked together. Glackens introduced Lawson to the patron Albert C. Barnes, who lived in the neighborhood and purchased works from both artists.

As with many of Lawson's works, the square is shown in winter. His preference for snow scenes originated in the early 1890s when he was a student of the American Impressionists John Twachtman and J. Alden Weir at the Cos Cob School in southeastern Connecticut. Lawson admired both painters but was stylistically influenced by Twachtman, whose winter scenes made his reputation. Like Twachtman, Lawson believed in painting out of doors but with a palette all his own. Typically, Lawson used more greens and reds, his signature colors, described by critic James G. Huneker as a palette of "crushed jewels."

ERNEST LAWSON (AMERICAN, 1873-1939), *Spring Scene*, N.D., OIL ON CANVAS, GIFT OF MRS. HUGH STALLWORTH, 1975.9.5 ALTHOUGH UNDATED, LAWSON'S RURAL SCENE IS CHARACTERISTIC OF THE SCENERY AT COS COB, CONNECTICUT.

ERNEST LAWSON (AMERICAN, 1873-1939) *View of Segovia*, C. 1916, OIL ON CANVAS, GIFT OF MR. AND MRS. WALTER KNESTRICK, 1986.16.16 LAWSON PAINTED IN SPAIN IN THE LATE TEENS WHERE HIS WORK TOOK ON A DARKER PALETTE.

PHOTOGRAPH OF ERNEST LAWSON, C. 1935. PHOTOGRAPHED BY PETER A. JULEY & SON. PHOTOGRAPHS OF ARTISTS COLLECTION I. ARCHIVES OF AMERICAN ART. SMITHSONIAN INSTITUTION

LILLIAN GENTH (AMERICAN, 1876–1953)

An elegant woman pauses on a sunny porch, looking down to touch summer flowers in a brass bowl. Lillian Genth's seemingly commonplace depiction contains symbols that suggest societal constraints encountered by turn-of-the-century American women. Her subject stands beside a wooden railing, a charming but continuous wall symbolically blocking her exit or the entrance of any other characters. Holding a red book, she absentmindedly plays with the flowers in a brass urn, her mind on other matters, possibly on what she has just composed in her diary. Genth relates the woman to the vase of flowers by painting both in the same palette: red, white, and green. Like the woman, the flowers are valued for their beauty. They have been cut from the garden growing on the other side of the railing and, so, are separated from the earth, just as the woman is in some sense separated from an aspect of her true nature.

Such constraint was not the case with Genth's favorite subjects, woodland nudes—a theme she first explored in Europe. Earlier in her career she had won a travel fellowship from the Pennsylvania Academy of the Fine Arts and, like most of her peers, had gone to France to study. But unlike the majority of her contemporaries—women like Ella Hergesheimer or Martha Walter—Genth chose to study overseas with James Abbott McNeil Whistler (1834–1903), an expatriate Impressionist whose flamboyant personality often overshadowed his art. Whistler fought the popular belief that all art must contain moral lessons. He believed that art had value as an aesthetic experience—radical thinking in Europe and, certainly, in conservative Philadelphia. It was in Europe, under Whistler's influence, that Genth's style and subjects changed. Assessing Genth's focus on the nudes, the critic Ada Rainey, a contemporary, notes that "a new and poignant realization of beauty came suddenly upon her. In this quick vision of the human form in the open, she had found her particular field of expression." Inspired by the combinations of light and texture found in her subject, and the natural association of humanity and nature, Genth returned to the woodland nudes throughout her career.

Lillian Genth made her living with portraiture and more traditional subjects, such as *Summer Afternoon*. In Rainey's estimation, the painting "represents the figure of a young girl in a charming flowered frock, intent upon flowers in a bowl on a table. The June sunshine streams through a green Venetian blind and irradiates the canvas with color." These were the subjects that appealed to turn-of-the-century patrons, and they were Genth's bread and butter.

ELLA S. HERGESHEIMER (AMERICAN, 1873–1943), *The Blue Jar*, N.D., OIL ON CANVAS, TRANSFER FROM THE NASHVILLE MUSEUM OF ART, 1960.2.13 LIKE GENTH, ELLA HERGESHEIMER STUDIED AT THE PENNSYLVANIA ACADEMY OF THE FINE ARTS, WHERE SHE, TOO, WON A TRAVELING SCHOLARSHIP TO PARIS.

PHOTOGRAPH OF LILIAN GENTH. PHOTOGRAPHED BY HAESELER. GEORGE WASHINGTON STEVENS PAPERS. ARCHIVES OF AMERICAN ART. SMITHSONIAN INSTITUTION.

Summer Afternoon, c. 1910, oil on canvas, Transfer from the Nashville Museum of Art, 1960.2.36

Rainbow, New York City, 1912, OIL ON CANVAS, GIFT OF THE 1992 COLLECTORS' GROUP WITH MATCHING FUNDS THROUGH THE BEQUEST OF ANITA BEVILL MCMICHAEL STALLWORTH, 1992.18

JOHN SLOAN (AMERICAN, 1871–1951)

Sloan painted at least five Manhattan rooftop scenes, two from his West Twenty-Third apartment, where he and his first wife, Dolly, set up housekeeping, and three (including this one) from his studio on the eleventh floor at 35 Sixth Avenue. His journal makes several references to the Sixth Avenue rooftop: "George Hamlin and Elizabeth called. I took them to the roof whence a fine view of the city can be had. 'Skyscrapers' piling up toward the southern end of N.Y. and scattered skyscraping buildings, not quite so much masses toward the North." (June 23, 1912).

Indeed, Manhattan's skyline first developed in the southern end of the city. At the turn of the century, land costs were highest ($300–$400 per square foot) in the financial district around Wall Street. Metropolitan Life Insurance Company, originally headquartered on lower Broadway, decided to make a statement when it built the Metropolitan Life Tower uptown in 1908. At over 700 feet, the structure held the title of tallest skyscraper in the world until 1913, when it was surpassed by Manhattan's 792-foot Woolworth Building.

Cheekwood's *Rainbow, New York City,* looks north up Sixth through Greenwich Village and past Union Square to Madison Square. The eye follows the receding avenue to the center of the background, where the old Metropolitan Life Building is partially framed by the arc of a rainbow, the biblical symbol of hope and promise. In 1912, skyscrapers were a recent phenomenon (following the invention of the electric elevator in 1880) and broadly accepted as heralds in their own right of a promising future.

Rosy, pearly, blue and brown,
Is the pale-washed sky;
Right and left, and up and down,
Gleaming roof-tops lie;

In the calm of autumn
All the city seems
A young giant dreaming
Fair and foolish dreams. . . .

–John Gould Fletcher, "Dominant City"

COMPARISONS:

JOHN SLOAN (AMERICAN, 1871–1951), *Roofs, Summer Night,* 1906, ETCHING, ARTIST'S PROOF, MUSEUM PURCHASE THROUGH THE BEQUEST OF ANITA BEVILL MCMICHAEL STALLWORTH, 1993.16 ONE OF SLOAN'S EARLIEST ROOFTOP SCENES IS FOUND IN THIS ETCHING FROM *THE CITY LIFE* SERIES, WHICH HE BEGAN IN 1905. HERE, THE SCENE IS A SUMMER'S EARLY MORNING ON A NEW YORK ROOFTOP, WHERE MANY TENEMENT DWELLERS SLEPT TO ESCAPE THE STIFLING HEAT.

JOHN SLOAN (AMERICAN, 1871–1951), *Sarah, Sally, Sadie, Peter and Paul,* 1915, OIL ON CANVAS, MUSEUM PURCHASE THROUGH THE BEQUEST OF ANITA BEVILL MCMICHAEL STALLWORTH, 1994.8 SLOAN SPENT HIS SUMMERS IN GLOUCESTER, MASSACHUSETTS, FROM 1914 TO 1917, DURING WHICH TIME HE EXPERIMENTED WITH A BRIGHTER PALETTE.

PHOTOGRAPH OF JOHN SLOAN, c. 1930. PHOTOGRAPHED BY PETER A. JULEY & SON. PHOTOGRAPHS OF ARTISTS COLLECTION II, ARCHIVES OF AMERICAN ART, SMITHSONIAN INSTITUTION.

JOHN SLOAN (AMERICAN, 1871-1951)
Portrait of Robert Henri, 1931, ETCHING, ARTIST'S
PROOF, MUSEUM PURCHASE THROUGH THE BEQUEST OF
ANITA BEVILL MCMICHAEL STALLWORTH, 1992.27
SLOAN, GLACKENS, AND ALBERT BARNES WERE
CLASSMATES AT PHILADELPHIA'S CENTRAL HIGH
SCHOOL. SLOAN AND GLACKENS WENT ON TO STUDY
AT THE PENNSYLVANIA ACADEMY OF THE FINE ART,
WHERE THEY MET ROBERT HENRI, WHO EVENTUALLY
SHARED A STUDIO WITH GLACKENS.

COMPARISON:

PHOTOGRAPH OF WILLIAM GLACKENS
AND HIS DAUGHTER, c. 1920.
PHOTOGRAPHS OF ARTISTS COLLECTION II.
ARCHIVES OF AMERICAN ART.
SMITHSONIAN INSTITUTION.

William Glackens spent the summer months of 1911–1916 at Bellport, New York, with his family and friends. The area had grown in popularity since the 1870s when the Long Island Railroad expanded its reach along the north and south sides of the island. In the early years of that decade, Bellport was still a simple village with a local ferry that shuttled bathers to the beach across the Great South Bay (weather permitting). Glackens's painting of sailboats on Long Island's Great South Bay could easily have been painted today. Although the area towns are now commercially developed, weekly boat races are still held during the summer months, sponsored by the Great South Bay Yacht Racing Association.

Bellport Regatta takes place before the race begins, when preparations are underway to ready the sailboats. In the background are sloops (in varying stages of readiness) and small "day sailers" (boats without below-deck sleeping accommodations) containing one main sail and one jib, their shaped, shallow hulls designed with a dropped centerboard or keel for maneuverability. The far-left boat has raised its mainsail and is coming into the wind while the boat to its immediate right is still tightening its jib, which looks a bit like an unstretched painting canvas. A vessel in the center distance is waiting for the race to begin. In the foreground, shuttle boats take passengers to waiting rigs. A dory, a double-ended boat, appears to have delivered its sailors and is returning to shore while at the far right a skiff with an outboard motor transports a team to their boat. The maneuvering of the boats and the bold pattern of the brightly colored waves accentuate the bustling activity that has begun to take place as the boats jockey for the best starting points.

The Glackenses spent a good part of their time at Bellport with Dr. and Mrs. Albert C. Barnes of Philadelphia. Dr. Barnes, who had grown wealthy in the patent medicine business, had contacted Glackens, his Central High School classmate, to help him acquire a collection of fine art. Just the year before, in 1912, Barnes had provided Glackens with $20,000 with which to visit Paris and buy art. With the artist Alfred Maurer as a traveling companion, Glackens visited numerous galleries, meeting Gertrude Stein and her brother Leo along the way. The Steins reintroduced Glackens to the work of the pioneer of Fauvism, Henri Matisse, first seen by Glackens at Alfred Stieglitz's gallery in 1908. Matisse's experiments with color would greatly influence Glackens, as seen in the bright purples, greens, and oranges in the waters of *Bellport Regatta*. Glackens's earliest beach scenes, painted at Coney Island between 1903 and 1907, have a darker tonality, reflecting Glackens's early tutelage under Robert Henri. Bellport's feathery brush strokes in the sky above the distant shoreline evoke the work of another Impressionist, August Renoir, whose method of paint application would dominate Glackens's canvases for the rest of his career.

Bellport Regatta, 1913, OIL ON CANVAS, MUSEUM PURCHASE THROUGH THE BEQUEST OF ANITA BEVILL McMICHAEL STALLWORTH, 1994.9

The Failure of Sylvester, 1914, OIL ON CANVAS, MUSEUM PURCHASE THROUGH THE BEQUEST OF ANITA BEVILL McMICHAEL STALLWORTH, 1993.6

ROBERT HENRI (AMERICAN, 1865–1929)

In the final stage of his career, Robert Henri often painted portraits in series, using the same model. During his stay in San Diego, Henri painted three portraits in 1914 of Sylvester, a local newspaper boy. In this series, Sylvester, at first sitting straight up, energetic, and smiling, gradually loses his battle with sleep after a long day of work and hours of posing for Henri. In *The Failure of Sylvester*, the final portrait of the series, Sylvester rests peacefully as Henri continues to work. In his earlier portraits, Henri typically used a dark, murky palette. However, in response to the bright California sunlight, Henri's color schemes, as in *The Failure of Sylvester*, become bright and colorful.

Henri, along with George Luks and John Sloan and other painters (critics derogatorily called them the Ashcan School), refused to be limited by the allegorical expression taught at the major art institutions. Henri and his colleagues painted subjects that were considered, by academic standards, unacceptable. Nineteenth-century European writers, such as Balzac and Tolstoy, who focused on working-class subjects and issues in their novels generated the themes that these urban realists fought to justify as legitimate subjects in the visual arts. *The Failure of Sylvester* continues in the thematic vein for which Henri had formerly been so bitterly criticized.

> *The people I like to paint are "my people," whoever they may be, wherever they may exist, the people through whom dignity of life is manifest, that is, who are in some way expressing themselves naturally along the lines nature intended for them.*
> —Robert Henri, *The Art Spiri.*

Sylvester lived during a period known as the Great Migration (ca. 1890–1940). Beginning with Reconstruction, and during the years of the Migration that followed, many African Americans left the poverty and desolation of the South to seek new lives in the booming industry of the North or the agricultural West, joining immigrants from Europe and Latin America. In households of the working poor, all able hands were needed to support the family; so children were frequently employed to supplement family income. Henri's Sylvester and his similar *Juan* were children from such families. They characterize the subjects that made Henri's reputation. His battle with the academic tradition won, Henri continued to focus on capturing the unique character in each sitter he chose to portray.

COMPARISON:

ROBERT HENRI (AMERICAN, 1865–1929), *Juan*, 1917, oil on canvas, Gift of the estate of John A. and Margaret Hill, 1994.19.35 Although painted in a much brighter palette, *Juan* resembles Sylvester with its large bravura brush strokes, working-class subject, and expression of the individual's personality.

PHOTOGRAPH OF ROBERT HENRI, c. 1897. Photographs of Artists Collection I. Archives of American Art. Smithsonian Institution.

WILLIAM JOHN WHITTEMORE
(AMERICAN, 1860–1955), *Sailor Girl,*
1910, OIL ON CANVAS, TRANSFER FROM THE
NASHVILLE MUSEUM OF ART, 1960.2.79
WHITTEMORE'S PORTRAIT OF A YOUNG GIRL
CONTAINS THE SAME CHARMING ATTRIBUTES THAT
MADE WALTER'S WORK SO POPULAR.

Martha Walter spent most of her career painting the two things she loved most, children and beaches. *Windy Day by the Sea* unites both themes in a sweetly sentimental scene. The location is Rocky Neck, an art colony in Gloucester Harbor, Cape Ann, Massachusetts.* Fitz Hugh Lane was the first-known artist to paint the area, in the 1840s. Many artists besides Martha Walter, including Winslow Homer, Childe Hassam, Maurice Prendergast, and John Singer Sargent, followed Lane to the harbor at Cape Ann. Around the period of World War I, Rocky Neck was Martha Walter's summer home. During the rest of the year, she often ventured from her New York City residence to paint nearby Coney Island and New Jersey's Atlantic City.

Walter developed her interest in beaches during a two-year tour of Italy, France, Spain, and Holland, sponsored by a Cresson traveling scholarship from the Pennsylvania Academy of the Fine Arts. She had studied in Philadelphia under the great teacher William Merritt Chase, who encouraged her to abandon the traditional method of drawing from antique plaster casts and to work independently. Walter met with success at the Academy, winning first the prestigious Toppan Prize in 1902 and, in 1908, the Cresson Prize. In 1910 she returned from Europe with sketches from the beaches of Deauville, Trouville, St. Malo, and Biarritz, where she had explored the French Impressionist penchant for outdoor or plein air painting. She carried this concept with her to New England's shores in *Windy Day by the Sea.*

Two young children standing on the shore dominate the painting. They have been looking across Gloucester Harbor at the activity taking place at the far pier. Two sailboats are visible, one with its sail up, another sail down. The boats are probably rushing to get out of an approaching storm, suggested by the fluttering ribbon in the girl's hair, the children's billowing clothes, and the ominously dark cloud in the upper register of the canvas. The children must have noticed the weather too, having returned from a walk in the country, evidenced by the boy's upturned hat full of just-picked yellow and pink flowers. Walter focuses her attention on the little girl's face. The child's large brown eyes and rosy cheeks are characteristic of Walter's portraits. Also typical is the warm palette, full of pinks and bright whites, and the loose brush stroke that Walter learned from Chase.

Windy Day by the Sea was an important work for Martha Walter. It was exhibited in New York at the Rochester Exposition and at the 109th Annual Exhibition of the Pennsylvania Academy of the Fine Arts in 1914. Eventually, the painting found its way into the collection of Mrs. Hugh Stallworth, one of Cheekwood's great benefactors, who donated the painting in her bequest. Walter continued to paint but rarely exhibited between 1930 and 1970. She produced an important series of forty-two paintings on the subject of Ellis Island in 1921 and 1922 but spent most of her time with friends and family in Philadelphia. Renewed interest in her work in the 1970s brought the limelight a second time, before her death in 1976 at age 101.

*ROCKY NECK IS ACTUALLY AN ISLAND, FOUNDED BY THE FRENCH EXPLORER CHAMPLAIN IN 1606. A CAUSEWAY WAS BUILT TO ACCESS THE ISLAND IN THE NINETEENTH CENTURY, FORMING ROCKY NECK AND THE INNER HARBOR. ROCKY NECK EXPERIENCED EXPLOSIVE GROWTH AFTER THE CIVIL WAR, FIRST AS A FISHING AREA AND, IN THE 1890s, AS AN ART COLONY.

PORTRAIT OF MARTHA WALTER
BY WILLIAM MERRITT CHASE, COURTESY DAVID
DAVID GALLERY, PHILADELPHIA, PA

Windy Day by the Sea, c. 1914, oil on canvas, Gift of Mrs. Hugh Stallworth, 1982.3.3

Top of Cape Ann Spring, 1918, OIL ON CANVAS, GIFT OF DR. AND MRS. ARMAND HAMMER, 1973.6.29

CHILDE HASSAM (AMERICAN, 1859–1935)

Childe Hassam's *Top of Cape Ann, Spring* is one of the artist's many exercises in color and light. The dappled patterning of flowers, rocks, and foliage provides an example of Hassam's self-proclaimed impressionistic practice of painting "light and air, and . . . full form in the light of day," while the bathing women contribute a voyeuristic mirage of classical imagery. Providing only a hint of sky, the sunset-lit *Top of Cape Ann, Spring* focuses on the fecundity both of the flowering bushes and of the women before them. The female figures, who are practically glowing with white-hued purity, exemplify Hassam's frequent use of nymphs–mythological spirits of nature who, in Hassam's paintings, serve as an homage to the classics and also reveal Hassam's keen interest in human nature.

Hassam, gifted with the ability to look simultaneously to history and to contemporary innovations for his influences, was a great advocate of painting for the sake of painting. Inspired by French Impressionism, which he encountered during studies at the Académie Julian in Paris during the 1880s, Hassam placed immense importance on the formal elements of light and color, writing in 1917, "The quality of color–and the quality of paint as a point to aim for is something." Although Impressionism's foremost concern with rendering an intimate impression rather than a realistic record played a major role in Hassam's art, he, unlike European Impressionist Claude Monet, did not abandon the figure or his love of classical imagery. As if marble statues of Aphrodite and Venus were carved into the New England landscape, the two figures in *Top of Cape Ann, Spring* strike poses similar to those of ancient Greek sculpture. Self-possessed in their activity, these bathers-turned-goddesses also seem to be unwitting objects of the artist's affection. This perspective turns viewer into voyeur, adding tension to the already spatially awkward placement of the women.

If the stiff, unrealistic, sculptural gestures of the figures also reveal Hassam's inconsistencies when rendering nudes, Hassam's defenders diverted attention back to color and light, which they emphasized as the essence of his work. As Adeline Adams said of Hassam, "As a seeker of light, more light, he chose his goal, and what he believed to be the best way to reach it."

LOUISE DAHL-WOLFE (AMERICAN, 1895–1989), *Night Bathing,* 1939, GELATIN SILVERPRINT, GIFT OF THE ARTIST, 1984.24.50

ELIHU VEDDER (AMERICAN, 1836–1923), *Nude,* N.D., CHARCOAL ON GRAY PAPER, GIFT OF DR. A. EVERETTE JAMES, JR., 1986.17.5

PHOTOGRAPH OF CHILDE HASSAM, 1913. Photographed by Caroline Reed Parson. Photographs of Artists Collection I. Archives of American Art. Smithsonian Institution.

COMPARISON:

CHARLES HAWTHORNE (AMERICAN, 1872–1930), *Portrait of a Student*, N.D., OIL ON CANVAS, GIFT OF DR. A. EVERETTE JAMES, JR., 1988.20.1 HAWTHORNE TAUGHT PALMER AND HIS OTHER STUDENTS THAT COLOR CONVEYED MORE OF THE CHARACTER OF A SUBJECT THAN DRAWING.

PHOTOGRAPH OF PAULINE PALMER
MEN & EVENTS: *Bulletin of the Union League Club of Chicago*, SEPTEMBER, 1939. PHOTO COURTESY OF THE ART INSTITUTE OF CHICAGO.

Family Gathering portrays eleven members of Pauline Palmer's family gathered on the porch of her home in seaside Provincetown, Massachusetts. Palmer maintained the home as a summer studio but spent most of the year in Chicago, where her husband worked as a physician and she was active in the local art community. Palmer gives us a sense of what was undoubtedly a scheduling feat in 1919 and brings us into the scene by placing a child in the immediate foreground. The restless little girl is captured chasing a ball, which appears to be rolling out of the painting's front edge. Her activity stirs the dog, looking for attention from someone in the preoccupied group. Palmer arranges her figures within the architectural frame of the porch, its white columns dividing the group into thirds. Two oriental rugs in the painting's center and background further define the groups, while a table separates foreground from background.

Family Gathering exhibits the characteristics that made Palmer one of the most popular society portraitists in turn-of-the-century Chicago. Short, controlled brush strokes enhance definition and draw the viewer's eye to the foreground subjects' faces, particularly the blonde child and the smiling woman at right. Note how the subjects lose definition as they recede into the background, so that the mother and children at the far end of the porch are unidentifiable. Palmer's loose brushwork in the clothes and architectural elements enliven the painting's surface, and her bright palette is accented with the sunny yellows that characterize many of her paintings.

Provincetown was an ideal location for painters of that period, who were attracted to the brilliant light and color of the area. Many of these artists had been exposed to French Impressionism while studying in Paris, and the tonalities of Provincetown suited their interest in tangible atmospheric effects. Situated near the end of the sandy cape, Provincetown became known as an artist colony in 1899, when the American Impressionist Charles Hawthorne established the Cape Cod School of Art. Students flocked to the cape where they learned to paint out of doors in the popular plein air manner of the French Impressionists. Pauline Palmer knew Charles Hawthorne and his influential teacher William Merritt Chase from her early studies in New York. She had also studied in Paris and in Italy both before and after her marriage, exhibiting six times at the Paris Salon between 1903 and 1911. Palmer was equally enthusiastic about Provincetown's resources and the visual and literary community that developed in the area.

After her husband died in 1920, Palmer spent much of her remaining eighteen years on Cape Cod. It was a place to find like-minded "conservative" painters (a term she would have proudly applied to her own work), who rejected the more abstract art forms that had taken root in America after the 1913 Armory Show. As the years passed, Palmer's Impressionistic style, so daring and avant-garde in the early 1900s, matured but never followed in the direction of the modernists.

Family Gathering, 1919, oil on canvas, Gift of the 1988 Collectors' Group with matching funds through the bequest of Anita Bevill McMichael Stallworth, 1988.16

Texas John Kelly, 1931, oil on linen, Gift of the estate of John A. and Margaret Hill, 1994.19.29

JOHN STEUART CURRY (AMERICAN, 1897–1946)

John Steuart Curry was born and raised on a farm in western Kansas. Although he spent the greater part of his life in urban environments, Curry made regular visits back to the farm to see family and friends. *Texas John Kelly* was probably painted on one of those trips. Its subject is one of the local cowboys, a noncommissioned portrait that Curry painted for his own pleasure or for future use in a larger project.

Beginning in the 1860s, cowboys like Texas John Kelly made regular passes through Kansas, during annual spring roundups or on the long cattle drives to shipping points. The cows were herded on routes like the Chisholm Trail through Oklahoma, past Wichita or Dodge City, to Kansas City's railroad yards. For Easterners at the time, Kansas City was the end of the line; for the cattlemen it was the western-most shipping point for cattle headed east. The combination of crowds and cattle produced an exciting spectacle, as noted in this first-hand report:

But I forgot to tell you about Kansas City. I never see nothin' like that railroad station in my life. Boy, it was a sight in them days. It was the gateway to the west, and there was more life and action there than there is in a dozen Grand Centrals. Trains was leavin' for everywhere, and the station was crowded with immigrants and their baggage, leavin for new homes and new lives. There was somethin' about it that was mighty thrillin'. It was a sight that won't be seen again in this country, and I never forgot it. Just hearin' the train hollerin' 'All Points West!' was a thrill for a greenhorn traveler like me. (Mr. Botsford on Travel-Kansas, December 27, 1938, oral history, Archives of American Art)

The hard life of the cowboy, both on the trail and on the range, is written on Texas John Kelly's face. These men were often on the trail for two months, herding as many as 1,500 head of cattle about twenty miles each day. They slept on the ground, which was often cold and wet, on a few quilts that they kept with their saddle, which served as a pillow. Exposed to the elements, cowboys had to be prepared for sudden changes in climate:

We were struck by a "Blue Norther" and the next thing it was sleeting. The wind was blowing so hard that it cut like a knife. I had to dig into the ground that night, to keep from freezing. (H. P. Cook, Rangelore, Cottle Co., oral history, Archives of American Art)

Curry painted the weathered face of this cowboy with great care, using his smallest brush strokes in that area that bore the brunt of the severe life. Flecks of blue suggest shadows in the roughened face, and red highlights on the left eye give Kelly a weary look. Unashamed of his worn features, Kelly stares out at us, the straight line of his mouth neither happy nor sad. Curry's broader brush strokes used for the cowboy's checked shirt, kerchief, and hat make plain that the story in the face is what captured his attention.

By the time *Texas John Kelly* was painted, Curry's student years were far behind him. His big break had come in 1928 when Mrs. Harry Paine Whitney saw his *Baptism in Kansas* at the Corcoran Gallery in Washington and gave Curry a support grant. After his work began to sell, Curry spent the remainder of his years painting and teaching at the Cooper Union, the Art Students League, and, finally, the University of Wisconsin, where he held the first artist-in-residence position in the U.S.

Curry painted scenes of the Midwest throughout his life and became known as one of the leaders of the Regionalist school of art. The Regionalists were a group of artists working during the Depression who painted nostalgic scenes of the West and Midwest as metaphors for American values. The three leaders of the group, Thomas Hart Benton, Grant Wood, and Curry, touched a chord among the country's politicians, who funded narrative murals by each under the Works Progress Administration (WPA).

COMPARISONS:

HARVEY JOHNSON (AMERICAN, B.1921) *Chowtime in Montana*, 1972, OIL ON CANVAS BOARD, GIFT OF MR. AND MRS. JOHN A. HILL, 1991.10.46 LIVING CONDITIONS FOR THE COWBOY WERE HARD. THE COOK OFTEN SCOUTED AHEAD OF THE HERD TO FIND A SUITABLE CAMPGROUND AND BEGIN DINNER PREPARATIONS.

THEODORE VAN SOELEN (AMERICAN, 1890–1964), *Cowboy's Day Off*, N.D., EGG TEMPERA ON PANEL, GIFT OF MR. AND MRS. JOHN A. HILL, 1991.10.42 VAN SOELEN SHOWS US A BRIEF MOMENT OF RESPITE IN THE COWBOY'S HARD LIFE.

PHOTOGRAPH OF JOHN STEUART CURRY. JOHN STEWART CURRY AND CURRY FAMILY PAPERS, 1897–1994, ARCHIVES OF AMERICAN ART. SMITHSONIAN INSTITUTION.

MILTON RESNICK (AMERICAN, B. 1917)

ALAN SARET (AMERICAN, B. 1944) *Toward Union Pleased*, 1982, STEEL AND NICKEL, GIFT OF MR. AND MRS. EUGENE JUDD, 1984.10.17AB

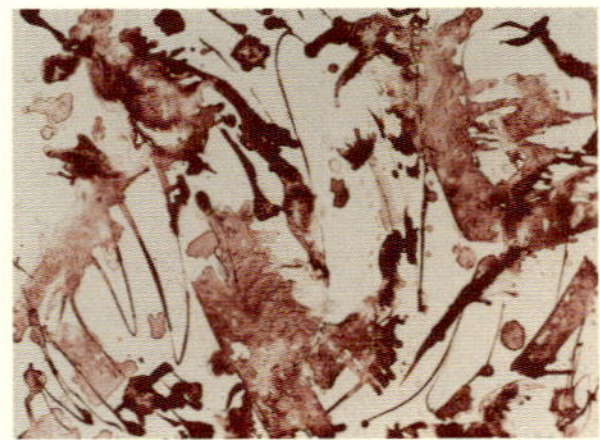

LEE KRASNER (AMERICAN, B. 1908-1984) *Pinkstone*, 1969, LITHOGRAPH ON PAPER, GIFT OF MR. AND MRS. RICHARD J. SCHAAP, 1979.12.11.3

MILTON RESNICK B.C. HOLLAND GALLERY RECORDS, 1959-1991. ARCHIVES OF AMERICAN ART. SMITHSONIAN INSTITUTION.

In 1957 Milton Resnick mused that he wanted his painting to "act in many different directions at once, so stingingly that it would open up a small crack, which will suck in the world." In this untitled work from 1958, Resnick created a painting that practically explodes with directional brush strokes and dramatic color, forming a composition that Harris Rosenstein has called "thoroughly personally inhabited." This early painting comes from Resnick's honest introspection in the service of a lifelong pursuit of personal style and from his effort to explore visual language through what the artist described as "the possibility of life in the paint itself."

With its thick layer of acrid color, Resnick's abstract seems to recall the childhood enterprise of finger painting—in William Seitz's words, Resnick's "free manipulation of pigment." With its confident and almost aggressive brush strokes, this painting resonates with the directional vigor of the crowded sidewalks and busy streets of New York, Resnick's home. In addition to reflecting the painter's environment, the painting reflects Resnick's admiration for friend and painter Willem de Kooning, who was already known for his flamboyantly guttural painting style.

Resnick, like many abstract painters during the 1950s, was further influenced by existentialism, which alleges that in a world full of catastrophe the only act of value is the formation of internal identity through self-creation. This credo spurred many artists of Resnick's expressionistic ilk to utilize art as a means of self-exploration. In this excerpt from an untitled poem Resnick touches on this quest for self-evolution:

The "business" of Resnick's career was not as effective in igniting the art world as was the influential first-generation Abstract Expressionists who preceded him. Resnick was, however, a vital member of the second-generation followers of that movement and a vital contributor to the 1950s New York School, a loosely constructed social community of New York artists influenced by de Kooning and fellow painter Hans Hofmann.

And steeled to last
A courteous and circumspect
Vision; it searches the Elect
That might yet reach a pale weightless stage
Poised for one hard diameter
To make them as strong as ethics were
or ethereal as Boehme's age.
If only we'd turn back to clay
From business, we might learn a way.

The young Resnick soon found his own artistic voice, taking a dramatic stylistic turn within one year of this painting's execution. His need to use the distinctive directional lines seen here diminished, while his admiration for Impressionist Claude Monet's equilibrium of composition surfaced. This shift was exhibited in Resnick's field paintings, in which imagery was treated equally throughout and provided none of the distinctive focal points of this early untitled work. As if Jackson Pollock's splatter paintings had collided head-on with the back-lit ambiance of Impressionism, Resnick's compositions lost the directionally charged energy of his early work and gained the encrusted uniformity of paint and texture for which he would become known.

Untitled, 1958, OIL ON PAPER, GIFT OF GRACE BORGENICHT BRANDT, 1984.21.21

Coke Break, 1960, OIL AND TEMPERA ON BOARD, GIFT OF DR. AND MRS. CHARLES E. WELLS, 1969.7

ISABEL BISHOP (AMERICAN, 1902–1988)

So I got to see that the only way I could convey anything of my vision was to . . . hardly create the figures in trying to suggest their being kind of a map of life. It's in the appearing and disappearing. . . .

—ISABEL BISHOP

Coke Break exemplifies Isabel Bishop's interest in the mundane movements and gestures of everyday life. Two women are shown here during a break from work, one taking her seat on a stool at a diner, the other already seated. Bishop painted her figures in a near transparent manner to suggest motion and action. She recorded a moment in transition and time, at once frozen yet continuing to move forward.

Overshadowed by the traditional social roles of the early twentieth century, women struggled to assert their independence. From the suffrage movement branched a widening array of occupational options as well as lifestyle choices for women like those in the painting. As with other occupations traditionally dominated by men, women artists also found difficulty gaining acceptance for their own artistic merits. In that challenging environment, at age sixteen in 1918, Isabel Bishop left home to study at the New York School of Applied Design for Women and to begin her career in commercial illustration. Shortly after her arrival, she discovered modern art and was so struck by its possibilities that she transferred to the Art Students League. There she studied primarily under Kenneth Hayes Miller, whose teaching reputation rivaled Robert Henri, a famous predecessor at the school. Miller grounded his own works in the early Renaissance tradition of linear modeling and bright colors, but focused on commonplace figures and everyday scenes. Although her style deviated from Miller's methods, she adopted his philosophy of emphasizing style before subject matter. Bishop also attended classes by Guy Péne du Bois, whom she admired for the refinement and vivacity of his paintings.

Isabel Bishop's career took flight during the 1930s, at a time when Regionalist art and abstraction were fierce competitors in the art scene. Throughout her life Bishop chose her subjects, as in *Coke Break*, based on the scenes of daily life she witnessed in New York's Union Square district. At one time, this neighborhood was filled with mansions, elegant department stores, and expensive restaurants accommodating some of the wealthiest New Yorkers. But in the 1920s Union Square became a business and industrial sector abounding with lower and middle-class men and women. Bishop and other artists located studios there, forming an artistic community that included Kenneth Hayes Miller and Reginald Marsh. Bishop's sketches of daily hustle and bustle, quickly drawn while riding on the subway, became the inspiration for finished paintings.

COMPARISONS:

ISABEL BISHOP (AMERICAN, 1902–1988)
Study for Coke Break, N.D., INK ON PAPER, GIFT OF THE ARTIST, 1969.6.11
ISABEL BISHOP PRODUCED DRAWINGS LIKE THESE TO INSPIRE AND COMPOSE THE CONTENT OF HER PAINTINGS. THE SPONTANEOUS, SKETCHY LINES, LIKE THOSE OF HER PAINTINGS, ILLUSTRATE MOVEMENT AND ACTION.

ISABEL BISHOP (AMERICAN, 1902–1988)
Study for Coke Break, N.D., INK ON PAPER, GIFT OF THE ARTIST, 1969.6.10

PHOTOGRAPH OF ISABEL BISHOP:
PETER A. JULEY & SON COLLECTION.
SMITHSONIAN AMERICAN ART MUSEUM.

COMPARISONS:

LARRY RIVERS (AMERICAN, B. 1923),
STUDY FOR *Dutch Masters,* N.D., LITHOGRAPH,
MUSEUM PURCHASE THROUGH THE BEQUEST OF ANITA
BEVILL MCMICHAEL STALLWORTH, 1994.23

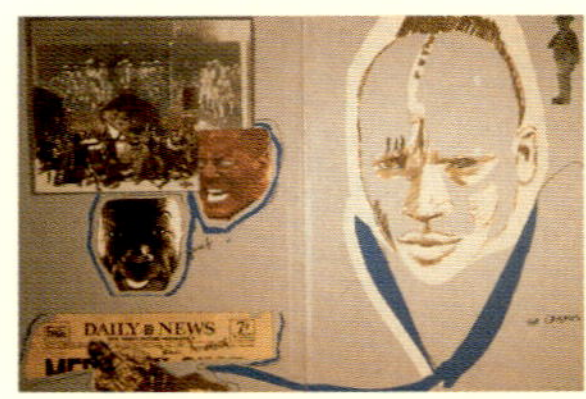

LARRY RIVERS (AMERICAN, B. 1923)
Black Revue FROM *The Boston Massacre*
SERIES, 1970, SCREENPRINT, ED. 56/150,
GIFT OF S.D. SOHACKI, 1979.12.14.6

PHOTOGRAPH OF LARRY RIVERS
ARCHIVES OF AMERICAN ART.
SMITHSONIAN INSTITUTION.

Larry Rivers successfully blended abstract art with realistic subject matter. Along with Jasper Johns and Robert Rauschenberg, Rivers helped to establish the visual segue from Abstract Expressionism to Pop Art. When Willem de Kooning and Jackson Pollock dominated the art world with their abstract, nonrepresentational paintings, Rivers deliberately challenged their standing. In *Dutch Masters I*, Rivers teasingly pays homage to Rembrandt, one of his favorite artists, who painted *The Syndics of the Cloth Guild* in 1662. The same image, however, also appeared on the popular Dutch Masters cigar box.

Dutch Masters I modernizes an "Old Masters" painting by infusing it with the painterly brush strokes of abstract art and written words, including the brand name, "Presidents," and "cigar." His blending of disparate forms created new sensations reinterpreting Old Masters art, much as Red Grooms did with his picto-sculpto-rama *Mr. and Mrs. Rembrandt*, also in the Cheekwood permanent collection.

Rivers began his professional career as a jazz musician. His paintings seem akin to the rhythms and improvisations of jazz. In addition Rivers has an ongoing fascination with historical narratives, a prime example of which can be seen in Cheekwood's *The Boston Massacre*, 1970. Despite this affinity for story telling, Rivers's work is purposefully fractured or jumbled. His paintings may be more closely related to the way the mind's eye perceives and processes life as it is experienced and remembered. In commenting on these processes and how he works, Rivers said, "In order to paint, I must look at something and I must think that in some way, the painting is about the thing I'm looking at as well as the process of looking."

Dutch Masters I, 1963, oil on canvas, Purchased with funds from the National Endowment for the Arts and matching donations from the following: Mr. Alvin G. Beaman; Bernal Foundation of Nashville; Mr. and Mrs. Martin Brown; Barbara Massey Clark; Dr. and Mrs. William Ewers; Exchange Club Charities; Mr. and Mrs. D. W. Johnson; Mr. Dortch Oldham; Dr. and Mrs. Robert Quinn; Mrs. Sara S. Stengel; Dr. and Mrs. Charles E. Wells, 1974.5.2

Untitled (Dutch Boy Diamond #5), 1965, ENAMEL ON LINEN, ANONYMOUS GIFT

ROBERT RYMAN (AMERICAN, B. 1930)

On the one hand, Robert Ryman approaches painting methodically—exploring how paint reacts to light and interacts with architecture—and, on the other hand, impulsively—creating tangible objects informed only by the moment they were created.

Guided by his intuitive impulses, Ryman creates paintings that respond to light by "using real light on real surfaces rather than creating an internal illusion of light," all the while being careful to observe "how real light acts upon those surfaces." Consequently, viewing a number of Ryman's paintings can be compared to observing the various incarnations of the ocean. Whereas the ocean's water is substantively consistent, like Ryman's paints, its texture changes with the wind and its surface hues with the time of day, creating mood-eliciting compositions as these elements vary.

Untitled (Dutch Boy Diamond #5), with its warm and smooth reflective surface, is one moment of time, one experiment during Ryman's thirty-year career. It is a quiet moment, a placid body of water, a ruminant reflector of light. But, most importantly, it is the tangible result of an artist's spontaneous response to paint.

Robert Ryman, who moved to Manhattan from Nashville to become a jazz musician, began his painting career when he walked into an art-supply store in the early 1950s:

I went in and bought some oil paint and canvas board and some brushes—they didn't have acrylic at that time—and some turpentine. I was just seeing how the paint worked, and how the brushes worked. I was just using the paint, putting it on a canvas board, putting it on thinly with turpentine, and thicker to see what that was like, and trying to make something happen without any specific idea what I was painting.

Ryman continued his art education by becoming a keen on-the-job observer while a security guard at the Museum of Modern Art, New York. After his first piece was exhibited in the 1958 MOMA staff exhibition, Ryman went on to explore the workings of twenty-five types of paint and thirty-one different types of supports, creating works that have been shown internationally in nearly five hundred exhibitions.

This painting, created early in Ryman's career, is one of a small group of canvases that was exhibited in his 1972 solo exhibition at the Guggenheim Museum in New York. Although the painting was created before Ryman began to use exposed wall fasteners as part of his compositions, the linen sides of this painting—which serve as an equally important, textured opposite to the smoothly-reflective, enamel face—foreshadow Ryman's unfaltering dedication to his own definition of realist painting:

With realism the aesthetic is an outward aesthetic instead of an inward aesthetic, since there's no picture there's no story. And there's no myth. And there's no illusion, above all. So lines are real, the space is real, the surface is real and there's interaction between the painting and the wall plane unlike abstraction and representation.

Believing that "it's part of the painter's task to expand our 'way' of seeing to the furthest limits of the painter's vision," Ryman invites the viewer to forget preconceived notions about painting and to see the medium, if only for a moment, as one way to create intuitively produced objects rather than illusionistic interpretations of reality.

JENNY HOLZER (AMERICAN, B. 1950), *Untitled (In a Dream)*, 1997, VERMONT WHITE MARBLE, MUSEUM PURCHASE WITH FUNDS PROVIDED BY VARIOUS DONORS THROUGH EXCHANGE, 1998.5

PHOTOGRAPH OF ROBERT RYMAN BY ROBERT E. MATES, COURTESY OF PACEWILDENSTEIN GALLERY, NEW YORK CITY, NY

ANDY WARHOL (AMERICAN, 1928–1987),
Miss Lillian, N.D., SILKSCREEN ON PAPER , GIFT OF
FRANK FOWLER AND TOM BEARD, 1977.12.77

Andy Warhol recalled preparing a discotheque for its opening in 1966, writing,

> *We brought down one of those big revolving speakeasy mirrored balls . . . We thought it would*
> *be great to bring those back. (The balls really caught on after we revived the look, and pretty*
> *soon they were standard fixtures in every discotheque you walked into.)*

This incident describes Warhol, an unerring barometer of his times, literally setting the stage for the 1970s. Influenced by the paparazzi glamour of that decade—by nightclubs such as Studio 54, the crisp photographs of Richard Avedon, and the shimmering, minimal gowns of Halston—Warhol's portraits from this period are characterized by obliterated facial contours and, in the words of art historian Robert Rosenblum, the acrid colors of his "new plastic spectrums of chemical hues both deadly and gorgeous."

It is no coincidence that as the superficial hues of celebrity life became hyped-up, Warhol's portraits grew more unctuous and unabashed. In *Portrait of Jamie Wyeth with Tan Background,* Warhol's treatment of Wyeth resonates with the same grandiosity as his celebrity portraits of Lana Turner and Elizabeth Taylor, elevating the visual artist into the stratosphere of super stardom. Striving to capture characteristics unique to each subject, Warhol's portrait of Wyeth pays thoughtful attention to the subject's facial expression and gesture. The placement of Wyeth's hand and his averted gaze portrays a pensive, perhaps shy, man. But Wyeth's solid thoughtfulness meets awkwardly with the garish scale, light, and hues of the artwork. The disco-inspired style of this portrait, coupled with Wyeth's demure demeanor, create a dramatic tension between the individuality of Wyeth and the growing American obsession with celebrity.

In an era when the commodity of the superstar was a burgeoning American business, it is not surprising that Warhol became, in Rosenblum's words, "a celebrity among celebrities, and an ideal court painter to this 1970s international aristocracy that mixed, in wildly varying proportions, wealth, high fashion, and brains." It is also not surprising that the man who said that "in the future everybody will be famous for fifteen minutes" breathed new life into portraiture after it was virtually ignored by an art world preoccupied with the purely formal concerns of abstraction.

Glamorous and powerful, the roster of Warhol's sitters eventually included such notables as gallery owner Leo Castelli, fashion designer Halston, actors Dennis Hopper and Liza Minelli, and rock star Mick Jagger. The majority of these paintings, like *Portrait of Jamie Wyeth with Tan Background,* stand today as testaments to Warhol's possession of what artist Barbara Kruger deemed an "acuity [that] can be construed as a kind of coolness; and [the] ability to collapse the complexities and nuances of language and experience into chilled silences of the frozen gesture."

PHOTOGRAPH OF ANDY WARHOL 1980.
PHOTOGRAPHED BY UGO MULAS.
PHOTOGRAPHS OF ARTISTS COLLECTION I.
ARCHIVES OF AMERICAN ART.
SMITHSONIAN INSTITUTION.

Portrait of Jamie Wyeth with Tan Background, 1976, ACRYLIC AND SILKSCREEN, MUSEUM PURCHASE WITH FUNDS PROVIDED BY THE FOLLOWING: MR. AND MRS. ROGER C. BUNTIN; MR. AND MRS. FRANK FOWLER; MARTIN HAYES AND CO., INC.; MAMIE C. HOWELL IN MEMORY OF CORINNE CRAIG OLIVER; MR. AND MRS. JACK C. MASSEY; NLT CORPORATION; IN MEMORY OF MR. AND MRS. JOHN OMAN, JR.; MR. AND MRS. JOE M. ROGERS; MRS. HUGH STALLWORTH AND AN ANONYMOUS DONOR., 1976.12.5

Portrait of Andy Warhol, 1976, OIL ON PANEL, MUSEUM PURCHASE WITH FUNDS PROVIDED BY THE FOLLOWING: MR. AND MRS. ROGER C. BUNTIN; MR. AND MRS. FRANK FOWLER; MARTIN HAYES AND CO., INC.; MAMIE C. HOWELL IN MEMORY OF CORINNE CRAIG OLIVER; MR. AND MRS. JACK C. MASSEY; NLT CORPORATION; IN MEMORY OF MR. AND MRS. JOHN OMAN, JR.; MRS. HUGH STALLWORTH AND AN ANONYMOUS DONOR., 1976.12.4

JAMES (JAMIE) WYETH (AMERICAN, B. 1946)

Jamie Wyeth creates portraits that in 1987 critic Lincoln Kirstein described as having "an almost hallucinatory impact and presence." That Wyeth's work possesses an other-reality quality echoes a review of *Portrait of Andy Warhol* printed a decade earlier:

Warhol and his dachshund Archie stare out at the viewer like Byzantine icons, frontal and unyielding . . . and the visceral feeling of the depicted flesh may indeed result from minute observation but Warhol looks for all the world like Lazarus raised from the dead.

Not only does this portrait boast a spectral presence, but it manifests Wyeth's tendency, as in his posthumous portrait of President John F. Kennedy, to provide the viewer with an unexpected, unfamiliar, and often vulnerable portrait. As Kirstein wrote, "[it is] almost as if Warhol had been caught off guard without his public persona."

The most striking of the aforementioned accomplishments in this portrait, however, is Wyeth's ability to portray an honest and vulnerable image of the legendary Andy Warhol. Wyeth transcends Warhol's public persona by presenting an exacting accumulation of external details that, through the use of tangible objects as clues, resonate with the internal traits of the subject. In *Portrait of Andy Warhol*, the subject's characteristically unbuttoned collar and loose tie allude to the side of Warhol that was happy amassing what Walter Hopps described as "a congested array of Americana" and was comfortable residing in a house that, in some rooms, contained "a sea of magazines covering the entire floor, ankle-deep, wall-to-wall. . . ." Warhol's agape mouth, an ironic characteristic of his seemingly indifferent public mask, speaks to Warhol's reputation for absorbing his environment without judgment or reservation.

After deciding over lunch at Manhattan's Elaine's restaurant to paint each other, Warhol and Wyeth embarked on a two-month sitting at Warhol's studio, The Factory. Warhol turned up for the sessions with his dog, a tape recorder, and his Polaroid camera. In describing the event, Wyeth said, "He never turned off the tape while we were working, and while I was painting he would be taking Polaroids of me." The pairing of these artists, with their virtually opposite styles, is not, according to Wyeth, as incongruous as it seems, "We aren't really as diametrically opposed as everyone seems to think. . . . Actually we both use representative forms in our art, and we work with everyday objects."

Warhol and Wyeth's most telling similarity, however, lies not so much in their use of the same objects as in their common selection of distinctly American subjects. Warhol's work, with its compulsive repetition of American products such as Coke bottles and soup cans as well as glamorous celebrities, such as Liz Taylor, Elvis Presley, and Marilyn Monroe, is the more obtrusive gatherer of unique Americana. Wyeth's paintings are based on his own more intimate America, which draws on his rural upbringing as the son of the popular American painter Andrew Wyeth, his love of animals, and his admiration for the great American artists Winslow Homer and Thomas Eakins. An early advocate of truly American subjects and style, Eakin argued that "if America is to produce great painters and if young art students wish to assume a place in the history of the art of their country, their first desire should be to remain in America to peer deeper into the heart of American life."

Warhol contemplated modernization's effect on our perceptions of what "American life" actually is, writing:

Everybody has their own America, and then they have pieces of a fantasy America that they think is out there but they can't see. . . . But you can only live in one place at a time. And your own life while it's happening to you never has any atmosphere until it's a memory. So the fantasy corners of America seem so atmospheric because you've pieced them together from scenes in movies and music and lines from books. And you live in your dream America that you've custom-made . . . just as much as you live in your real one."

Warhol and Wyeth together represent the joining of the "dream" America of Hollywood, advertising, and Rock-n-Roll with the "real" America of rural topography, animals, friends, and family. *Portrait of Andy Warhol* demonstrates Wyeth's ability to permeate the dream Andy Warhol—the Warhol legend created by admirers and detractors alike—and arrive, through precise and personal observation, at the truth beyond the legend.

VALERIE FUSSELL (AMERICAN, LATE 20TH CENTURY), *Self-Portrait, Flanders,* 1992, ACRYLIC ON BOARD, CHEEKWOOD NATIONAL CONTEMPORARY PAINTING COMPETITION PURCHASE AWARD WINNER THROUGH THE BEQUEST OF ANITA BEVILL MCMICHAEL STALLWORTH AND THE SERVICE MERCHANDISE–ZIMMERMAN FAMILY FOUNDATION, 1992.10

PHOTOGRAPHY OF JAMES (JAMIE) WYETH
PHOTOGRAPHED BY RICHARD FARRELL.

DALE KENNINGTON (AMERICAN, B. 1935)

BILL SAWYER (AMERICAN, LATE 20TH CENTURY), *Falls City,* N.D., OIL ON PANEL, GIFT OF MRS. WALTER SHARP, 1974.7.23

In *Style*, Dale Kennington created an image that focuses on communal habits and rituals. The painting is thoughtfully composed: a balance of pervasive riveting patterns, on the one hand, and, on the other, a by-play of tension and ease found, respectively, in the placement and gestures of the men. As in all of her paintings, Kennington, who painted this barbershop three times, tried, in art curator Peter Baldaia's words, to "give the viewer a lot of information . . . by indirect means, and then [allowed] the viewer to relate the painting to his or her own experience." One of Kennington's most arresting assets is her ability to treat visual style and the substance of her content equally.

Style's visual strength is the result of compositional tension in the treatment of light, shadow, and other formal elements, such as color and pattern. The juxtaposition of elements in *Style* reaches the level of elaborate pun: the literal fashion dispersed in the barbershop against the formal structure; the repeated patterns of stripes and checkerboard blocks; the stylized nature of the painting itself. Kennington, who paints from photographs, uses her own snapshots as a compositional reference for her paintings. Expounding on Kennington's method of building a composition, Baldaia writes, "In creating her paintings, Kennington employs a camera as what she terms a 'rapid-fire sketchbook,' often grouping and altering many different photographs to suit particular compositional aims."

Kennington's philosophical aim is driven by her central, deeply held belief that, as she says, "our lives are ultimately shaped not by the few cataclysmic events that happen to each of us, but by the everyday things we do," inspiring her to choose subject matter such as women trying on clothes in a dressing room, an elderly woman's birthday party, and rows of parents and children seated on bleachers at a swim meet. Kennington, consequently, exhibits a long-standing and effective artistic tradition of finding the universal in the specific, of relishing the communion that binds us in the repeated events of our daily lives. *Style* follows in this vein by portraying the universal ritual of grooming amid the defined setting of a small, Southern barbershop.

Kennington's skill of capturing the telling but undramatic event is one often used in photography, most notably by photographer Henri-Cartier Bresson, who concisely describes this phenomenon as "the decisive moment." By not capturing her decisive moments with one photograph but scrupulously constructing imagery using collage and imagination, many of Kennington's paintings take on a dream-like quality. The artist's use of a realistic painting style for concocted scenarios propels her imagery into a limbo between the social realism of painters such as John Sloan and the surrealism of artists like Réne Magritte.

This loyalty to the reality of her own vision has inspired the artist to use up to forty different photographs to create one composition. Kennington's *Style* transforms the actual barbershop—which is, according to Kennington, a square, all black-and-white room, into an infinitely reflected and profusely patterned arcade of imagery and color. This setting is created to serve as a visually loaded backdrop for the human characters it surrounds. The barbershop of Kennington's *Style* is, like all of her backdrops, a canvas onto which human drama unfolds, suggesting that Kennington would heartily agree with poet W. H. Auden, who once mused,

PHOTOGRAPH OF DALE KENNINGTON
COURTESY OF THE ARTIST.

To me, art's subject is the human play And landscape but a background to a torso.

Style, 1994, oil on canvas, Cheekwood National Contemporary Painting Competition Purchase Award Winner, through the bequest of Anita Bevill McMichael Stallworth and the Service Merchandise–Zimmerman Family Foundation, 1994.28

DETAIL: FLIGHT (ENGLISH, ACTIVE 1783–1792) *Plate*, 1792, FROM THE HOPE SERVICE, PORCELAIN, MUSEUM PURCHASE THROUGH THE EVERS ACQUISITION FUND, 1983.8.4

The most beautiful thing we can experience is the mysterious. It is the source of all true art and science.

Albert Einstein

CRAFTSMAN UNKNOWN, ENGLISH, GEORGIAN

Eighteenth-century Georgian architecture and interior design actually had its genesis much earlier in the late sixteenth and early seventeenth centuries with the work of Inigo Jones and Sir Christopher Wren. Jones was important to English architecture and design not for originality, but for introducing Jacobean England to the classical architecture and interiors of Andrea Palladio and ancient Rome. As surveyor to the royal family, Jones made several trips abroad, the second of which took him to Northern Italy. There he was able to study first hand Palladio's villas and their decoration, integrating their precepts into his own work.

By 1700 English architecture and design had moved from the church-influenced Gothic style to the more human-oriented neoclassical styles of Jones and Wren, who looked to the Italian Renaissance and to the ancient world. By mid-century, the designs of architect Robert Adam had enhanced this trend. While the Palladian influence is evident in his architecture, his interiors owe more to Etruscan wall paintings found during the excavations at Herculaneum, Pompeii, and ancient Rome.

This new style of architecture required revitalization of furniture design. Heavy, complex Gothic furniture gave way to the lighter and more ordered designs of Thomas Chippendale and Thomas Sheraton. French and German influence is seen in the overlaid gesso and graceful Rococo designs used for carved console tables, chairs, and stools.

This console table combines rococo and neoclassical influences. Expertly carved, the eagle was a common form in Etruscan and Roman furniture and also in the decoration of Palladian villas. An Etruscan-influenced curvilinear design on the table's entablature is taken from dados of wall paintings at Herculaneum and Pompeii. The ornamentations of gesso and gilt show the influence of eighteenth-century French and German rococo furniture designs that rely heavily on these two components. The marble top would have complimented the stone floors used in Georgian architecture.

Eagle Console Table (One of a pair), N.D., MAHOGANY, GESSO, GILT AND MARBLE, GIFT OF MR. LESLIE CHEEK, JR., 1985.8.1

Set of Four Hinged Medicine Bottles, 18TH CENTURY, ENAMELED METAL, GIFT OF MRS. JOSEPH THOMPSON, 1958.1.58

CRAFTSMAN UNKNOWN, CHINESE

Native Americans cultivated the tobacco plant for centuries before Europeans embarked for the North American continent in the late fifteenth century. After Europeans arrived and settled in the New World, commercial development of tobacco spread to the rest of the world through various European trade routes. By the late sixteenth century, the Japanese began planting and using tobacco, later trading it for goods in China during the seventeenth century. The Chinese used tobacco in a finely ground form called snuff, which was inhaled through the nose aided by a miniature spoon. Consumers often added scented substances to enhance and diversify the flavor. During the late seventeenth century, the snuff bottle was crafted as a portable snuff container that could easily fit into a pocket.

At first, only men and women of the court could afford snuff, but over time its use spread to the general public in a cheaper, less pure form. After popular acceptance of snuff grew throughout the first hundred years of the Ch'ing Dynasty (1644–1912), snuff survived attempts by opponents during the mid-seventeenth century to ban it. Ch'ien-lung (1736–1796), the fourth emperor of the Ch'ing Dynasty, and others in his court began amassing snuff bottles for their exquisite beauty and variety of shapes, sizes, and materials. These bottles became so valuable that they were often used as gifts to curry political favor. By 1900, snuff and snuff bottles were still part of everyday Chinese customs. Even in average homes, snuff was often offered to friends as a courteous gesture. After the collapse of the Ch'ing Dynasty, snuff usage sharply declined, essentially disappearing by 1949 in the wake of the Communist revolution. Between 1950 and 1960, snuff-bottle manufacturing was revived, primarily for the benefit of tourists and collectors.

This eighteenth century medicine bottle has four compartments and may have doubled as a snuff bottle. The hinges allow for folding and easy carriage in a pocket. Its molded metal body and enameled surface form figures and outdoor scenes.

COMPARISONS:

CRAFTSMAN UNKNOWN, CHINESE
Snuff Bottle, LATE 19TH CENTURY, GLASS,
GIFT OF MRS. JOSEPH THOMPSON, 1958.1.150
INTERIOR-PAINTED SNUFF BOTTLE: MANY SNUFF BOTTLES WERE DECORATED WITH PAINT. TO PROTECT THE DESIGN FROM CHIPPING BECAUSE OF FREQUENT USE, ARTISANS PAINTED THE INTERIOR OF THE BOTTLES (LIKE THIS ONE) THROUGH THE SMALL OPENING WITH A BAMBOO BRUSH. OWNERS SOMETIMES REMOVED THE SPOON ATTACHED TO THE LID FOR FEAR OF SCRAPING THE PAINTING; FREQUENTLY, SUCH BOTTLES WERE ACQUIRED PURELY FOR DISPLAY.

CRAFTSMAN UNKNOWN, CHINESE
Snuff Bottle, 18TH CENTURY, GLASS,
GIFT OF MRS. JOSEPH THOMPSON, 1958.1.126
OVERLAY SNUFF BOTTLE: ARTISANS OFTEN CREATED SNUFF BOTTLES FROM BLOWN GLASS. SEVERAL LAYERS OF GLASS OF DIFFERENT COLORS COULD BE APPLIED TO THE INITIAL STRUCTURE AND THEN CHIPPED AWAY TO CREATE COLORFUL, RELIEF DESIGNS.

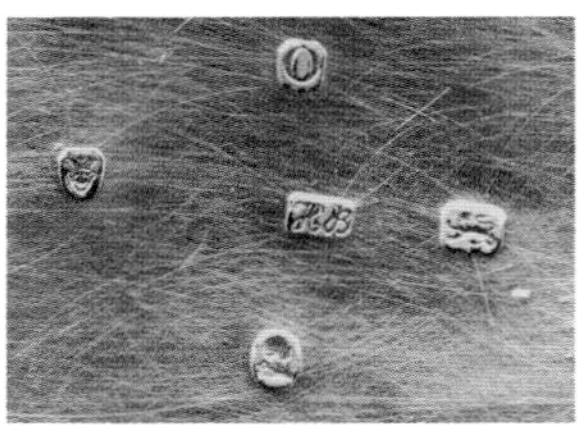

HESTER BATEMAN (ENGLISH, 1709–1794), *Tea Service (detail)*, c. 1785–90, THIS CLOSE-UP SHOWS THE MARKINGS ON THE BOTTOM OF THE PITCHER.

CRAFTSMAN UNKNOWN, GEORGIAN STYLE, TEAPOT, c. 1830, SILVER, GIFT OF MR. AND MRS. RUSSELL SPEIGHTS, 1970.11.26

COMPARISONS:

The spirit of the tea hour seems to be indelibly associated with England, for in no other corner of the world is this simple function still preserved with such dignity and care.
—SEYMOUR B. WYLER, *The Book of Old Silver*

Ever since the introduction of tea to England in the seventeenth century, the British have taken tea drinking and the almost ceremonial process surrounding its consumption quite seriously. When brought to the English court by the Chinese in 1664, tea leaves were rare in Europe and, consequently, extremely expensive. By the 1720s, demand for tea grew, importation increased, and prices eventually dropped, allowing this luxurious drink to be less exclusive. As more people made sipping tea a part of their everyday life, the necessity arose for appropriate vessels in which to serve the drink and the accompanying sugar and cream, additions to tea enjoyed by the British. Silversmiths were called upon to produce teapots, creamers, sugar baskets, teacups, teakettles, and a variety of other instruments involved in the tea ritual. The tea caddy, or canister, was an especially important container used to store precious teas and was often locked against children and servants. Proving that the decorative arts eventually reflect the customs and manners of the culture, virtually every English home of substance could claim a tea service by the end of the eighteenth century.

As the British palate was becoming increasingly fond of tea, Europe was experiencing a great revival of interest in ancient Greece and Rome, largely fueled by the discovery and excavation of Herculaneum in 1738 and Pompeii in 1755. European architecture, fashion, painting, and sculpture quickly adopted the orderly and simple classical style and borrowed elements seen on classical objects, such as urns, swags, floral motifs, and shields. This neoclassical style was made especially popular in England by the architect and designer Robert Adam, who traveled to Rome before becoming an influential court architect. Many British artisans, including Hester Bateman, welcomed the neoclassical style's return to order and simplicity after the flamboyant and undisciplined rococo period (see Bateman tea service, opposite page). Rather than through ornate, applied decorations, beauty was achieved through symmetry, graceful lines, and a two-dimensional simplicity that allows the forms and material to shine more clearly. In the Bateman tea service, the five pieces are based on a geometric, octagonal form with a straight spout, simple wooden handle, and gently curving scalloped edges. Extraneous ornamentation was reduced to subtle engraving of banded stars and crests inside a cartouche, all classical motifs. In this method of low-relief etching, called bright-cutting, light reflects off the facets of incisions, creating a soft glittering effect, again emphasizing the beauty of the material and simplicity of the lines and proportion.

The marks stamped on the bottom of each vessel provide clues to the history of the piece. For instance, five small marks can be seen on the teapot (see top left illustration). The mark depicting the profile of a man's head indicates that the silversmith paid his duty, or tax, to the reigning king, in this case, George III. The letter "K" signifies the date range 1789–1790. Next to the "O" stamp is the lion passant, the first known hallmark (introduced in 1300) to regulate the quality of silver and to protect the purchaser from fraud. The crowned leopard head was adopted as the official seal of the London Goldsmiths Hall in 1544. To this day, all pieces of silver made in London must have this stamp. The final stamp on the teapot is perhaps the most informative. The initials "HB," the maker's mark, tell the owner that Hester Bateman was the silversmith responsible for the piece's quality of craftsmanship and honesty in materials.

Hester Bateman registered her own maker's mark with the London Goldsmiths in 1761 upon the death of her husband in order to continue his business. This accomplished woman also trained her children to become skilled craftsmen, and by the 1780s the Bateman company held a solid reputation for high-quality, elegant designs. Mrs. Bateman continued working until her retirement in 1790 at the age of eighty-one, widely recognized as one of England's finest silversmiths. The Cheekwood tea set is an excellent example of the distinguishing characteristics of her work: extraordinary craftsmanship that combines graceful line and classical simplicity.

Tea Service, c. 1785–90, sterling silver, Gift of Mrs. Lula Woosley in memory of her husband W. Bryant Woosley, 1985.25.1–5

BARR, FLIGHT AND BARR (English, active 1804–1813), *Cream Jug*, 1805, From George III Service, porcelain, Gift of Dr. and Mrs. William Ewers, 1984.26.6

FLIGHT, BARR AND BARR (English, active 1813–1840), *Stowe Tureen*, 1812–1813, From the Stowe Service, porcelain, Gift of Mrs. Wayne T. Delay and Mr. William T. Delay in memory of Wayne Tilden Delay, 1988.2

FLIGHT, BARR AND BARR (ENGLISH, ACTIVE 1813–1840)
BARR, FLIGHT AND BARR, (ENGLISH, ACTIVE 1804–1813)

Dinner in Georgian England was not simply a meal but a ritualized event. In aristocratic households, dinner was typically composed of two or three courses of over twenty dishes each and could last up to five hours. Food was arranged on the table and sideboard for each course with an eye to a visually pleasing meal and with elaborate serving pieces of silver and porcelain to display the host's wealth and social prominence.

The great country houses of the Georgian English aristocracy were built with the dining room and its decoration taking on new importance as symbols of the owner's wealth and status. Under the influence of architect Robert Adam, the placement of the dining room was moved to the front, giving it equal prominence with the drawing room and allowing for ease of movement between the two for social occasions. Also under Adam's influence, the décor of the room moved away from the heavy tapestries and brocade wall coverings of earlier times to the lighter, neoclassical designs favored by the French and Germans.

The opening of the trade route to China in the 1600s made true porcelain available for the first time, replacing the heavier stoneware of previous centuries. Wares painted with chinoiserie patterns were highly prized. For generations the English placed orders with the Chinese for dinner services decorated with the owner's coat of arms. It was not until the 1740s that English porcelain factories developed a formula that could produce these delicate wares. The Worcester Porcelain Works started manufacture in 1751 and was the first of the English factories to develop a formula for true porcelain. Worcester began competing not only with the Chinese but with the European porcelain factories of Meissen and Sevres, whose designs were already popular among the English aristocracy.

Worcester first concentrated its manufacturing on tea wares but soon moved to specializing in elaborate dinner services and presentation pieces. Porcelain was manufactured in Worcester under numerous factory names–Dr. Wall; Flight; Flight and Barr; Barr, Flight and Barr; Flight, Barr and Barr; Chamberlain's; and, finally, the Royal Worcester factory, which is still in production today.

The Flight factory was the first of the Worcester factories to achieve success, with a tea service commissioned by the Duke of Clarence in 1792. The decoration of that service is elaborate but restrained, the only color coming from its gilding. By 1813, the date of this tureen from a Stowe Service commissioned by the Duke of Buckingham, the Flight, Barr and Barr factory had evolved to the neo-classical designs in vogue after the excavations at Herculaneum and Pompeii. Each piece of the Stowe service is painted with the full arms and supports of the Marquis of Buckingham. The rich orange ground and soft honey gilding were trademarks of the Flight, Barr and Barr factory. This tureen, which is part of the original dinner and dessert service, would have been used during the first course of dinner to serve soup, which, along with boiled meats, was a featured element of the course.

During a visit to Worcester in 1788 King George III and Queen Charlotte began the royal family's long history of patronage of local porcelain production. The couple purchased a dessert set from the Flight factory in the Blue Lily pattern. The pattern was renamed the Royal Lily pattern in honor of the royal couple. In 1805 George III ordered a complete dinner and dessert service from the Barr, Flight and Barr factory. The elaborate service is painted with the full royal coat of arms and is bordered by a deep-blue ground gilded with oak leaves and the royal cipher. This creamer, part of that original service, would have been used typically at the close of the Georgian dinner or with the breakfast service of tea or coffee.

COMPARISONS:

CHAMBERLAIN (ENGLISH, ACTIVE c. 1791–1851), *Meat Platter,* 1815–1820, PORCELAIN, GIFT OF DR. AND MRS. BENJAMIN H. CALDWELL, JR., 1979.1.3

FIRST PERIOD (WORCESTER, ENGLISH ACTIVE 1751–1774), *Teapot,* c. 1770, QUEEN CHARLOTTE PATTERN, PORCELAIN, GIFT OF MRS. MARTIN S. BROWN, 1981.6.1AB

FLIGHT (ENGLISH, ACTIVE 1783–1792), *Plate,* 1792, FROM THE HOPE SERVICE, PORCELAIN, MUSEUM PURCHASE THROUGH THE EWERS ACQUISITION FUND, 1983.8.4

FLIGHT (ENGLISH, ACTIVE 1783–1792), *Dish,* c. 1785, ROYAL LILY PATTERN, PORCELAIN, GIFT OF DR. AND MRS. BENJAMIN H. CALDWELL, JR., 1991.7

COMPARISONS:

TENNESSEE CRAFTSMAN UNKNOWN,
AMERICAN, *Sideboard,* c. 1815 (DETAIL)

decorative arts

CRAFTSMAN UNKNOWN, ENGLISH, IN THE
MANNER OF THOMAS SHERATON,
Sideboard, 1790-1800, MAHOGANY, GIFT OF
MRS. WALTER SHARP, 1974.7.1

CRAFTSMAN UNKNOWN, INDIAN EXPORT,
IN THE MANNER OF THOMAS
CHIPPENDALE, *Kneehole Desk,* c. 1775,
MAHOGANY, GIFT OF MRS. P. M. ESTES, JR., 1974.1.1

The earliest "side boards" were simple tables placed to the side of dining tables to hold serving dishes for the meal. By the mid-eighteenth century, drawers and narrow chambers were added to the sideboard to store silver and linens.* Cheekwood's sideboard was made of solid cherry with cherry, mahogany, and elm veneer. Built around 1815, it carries the characteristics of the popular Sheraton style (1795–1820) in its classic, elegant form, turned legs, segmental curves, and emphasis on inlay. Its brass drawer pulls, probably a later addition, display the image of Thomas Jefferson, who served as the country's president at the time of the sideboard's production.**

The Sheraton style was named for Thomas Sheraton (1751–1806), an English cabinetmaker and furniture designer, as well as the author of the popular design book *The Cabinet-Maker and Upholsterer's Drawing-Book,* a primer that introduced to America new elegant furniture designs. Such pattern books were an important means of communicating European design to American furniture designers and craftsmen.

Cheekwood's sideboard strongly resembles furniture made in Middle Tennessee in the early 1800s. Tennessee cabinetmakers combined extraordinary skill with elements of national and regional design to create distinct pieces of furniture. While imported mahogany was available, a number of sideboards were made from local hardwoods such as cherry. Surviving sideboards show the same use of a figured cherry veneer on the doors and drawer fronts. The overall construction and decoration of the piece testify to the expertise of its maker. The swelled front over recessed cabinets, the concave drawers on either side, and the use of inlay and veneer required more skill and more labor by the maker. As a result, the sideboard was a valuable piece of furniture in a household as well as a masterpiece of the craft.

*OTHER EIGHTEENTH-CENTURY INVENTIONS INCLUDE THE CHEST OF DRAWERS, GATE-LEG AND DROP-LEAF TABLES, AND UPHOLSTERED ARM CHAIRS.

** DURING HIS PRESIDENCY, JEFFERSON EXPERIMENTED WITH INTERNATIONAL CUISINE AND TOOK A KEEN INTEREST IN THE RANGE OF KITCHEN PRODUCTION FROM THE PLANTS GROWN IN THE GARDEN TO RECIPES USED AT HIS TABLE. HE EVEN INVENTED THE DUMBWAITER, WHICH ENABLED HIS GUESTS TO RECEIVE WARM FOOD BUT KEPT THE SERVANTS OUT OF THE ROOM, ALLOWING FOR PRIVATE CONVERSATION.

Sideboard, c. 1814, cherry with mahogany and elm inlay, Gift of Mr. and Mrs. O. W. June, 1976.7.2

Epergne, 1865, STERLING SILVER, GIFT OF MRS. WALTER SHARP, 1983.5.4–7

HUNT AND ROSKELL (ENGLISH, LONDON, ACTIVE 1844-1928)

The industrial revolution gave rise to a shift in the economic base of English society. Established fortunes based on agrarian society were superseded by industrial fortunes. Many of the older aristocratic families found themselves having to liquidate valuable household items to maintain their estates. This need for a practical method of liquidation led to the establishment of auction houses, which for the first time exhibited to the general public the masterpieces of early silversmiths. These auction previews inspired a new generation of silversmiths to design silver wares for the rising bourgeoisie. Such revivals of designs from previous eras had occurred as far back as the Italian Renaissance.

The industrial revolution changed the way silver and decorative objects were manufactured. Now no longer limited to hand craft, manufacturers offered machine-made wares to the middle class, household items once available only to the upper classes. By the mid-nineteenth century the London silversmith trade had evolved from small shops run by highly skilled master silversmiths to large incorporated firms employing many craftsmen. Only the very wealthy could afford the production of the few specialized shops devoted to hand-crafted silver inspired by the designs of such masters as Paul Crepsin, Paul de Laramie, and Paul Storr.

John Hunt & Company was one of several such specialized shops during the mid-nineteenth century. Apprenticeships with established silversmiths were required to obtain a license to manufacture silver, and Hunt had served his apprenticeship with Paul Storr. This explains the presence of Storr's mark on the epergne along with Hunt's, even though Storr had died twenty-one years earlier. Stylistically, the epergne reflects the influence of Storr's large presentation pieces. Also evident is the idea of nature in art, in the French manner that was being revived in English craftsmanship through a new wave of silversmiths working in England, much as the Huguenot silversmiths in the eighteenth century influenced English design. Two larger pieces were added to this epergne by the Barnard firm in the late nineteenth century.

The epergne came into common use during the Georgian era for dessert service at the dining table. Its use evolved to include sweetmeats for the main courses. By the Victorian era it was used also to hold decorative floral arrangements on both the dining table and sideboard.

CHAMPION (ENGLISH, BRISTOL, ACTIVE 1749–1957), *Pair of Gardeners*, c. 1775, PORCELAIN, MUSEUM PURCHASE THROUGH THE BEQUEST OF ANITA BEVILL MCMICHAEL STALLWORTH IN HONOR OF MRS. WILLIAM J. TYNE, 1992.26.2

ELKINGTON AND CO. (ENGLISH, BIRMINGHAM, c. 1829-1968, *Epergne,* 1877, STERLING SILVER GIFT OF MS. TENNIE MCGHEE, 1983.19

decorative arts

The works of prolific and innovative designer Louis Comfort Tiffany perhaps most clearly represent the Art Nouveau period, a style of design that dominated aesthetic taste around the turn of the century. This decorative style is characterized by fluid, sensuous curves often based on abstracted forms seen in nature, such as vines and flowers. In reaction to the mass-produced, often mechanical looking commodities manufactured during and after the industrial revolution, artists of this period were more interested in creating unique, well-crafted objects of beauty that pleased the connoisseur's eye. In the spirit of the Gilded Age, wealthy Americans wanted to create homes as opulent as those of the European aristocracy to display and promote their own status and taste. Objets d'art, including art glass, therefore, were appreciated for their appearance rather than for their function. The Tiffany vase in Cheekwood's collection, hand-blown circa 1899-1928, with its delicate, flaring trumpet form, colorful leaf motifs, and warm golden tone exemplifies this luxurious and elegant style.

Tiffany, the son of Charles L. Tiffany—founder of the still-popular store of Tiffany & Co. in New York—became interested in art at an early age. He studied at the National Academy of Design, took lessons with American painter George Inness, and traveled extensively to view the artistic treasures of Europe, North Africa, and the Near East. His trips to the Near East, where, as he described, "the pre-eminence of color in the world was brought forcibly to my attention," had an especially profound effect on the young Tiffany's later style and techniques. He "returned to New York wondering why we made so little use of our eyes." Tiffany's love of the colorful and unconventional evolved into a style that married Eastern and Western aesthetics while combining fine art and utilitarian craft. As his focus shifted more toward interior design, he also began to see an artistic nobility in the craftsmanship of the decorative arts. Tiffany claimed,

Many painters and sculptors began as craftsmen. The latter are nearer the people, for they fabricate useful objects belonging to daily life, while the artist who produces objects of the fine arts, so called, is more remote. His work usually demands on the part of the observer a longer education for its appreciation. . . .

Already respected for the quality and design in his leaded glass windows, lampshades, and mosaics, in 1893 Tiffany became interested in exploring the properties and possibilities of blown glass. He began experimenting with new techniques in his furnace in Corona, New York, in order to create unique vessels with innovative colors, surfaces, textures, and levels of translucence. His experiments ultimately resulted in a new type of glass characterized by a satiny finish and rich, iridescent colors, like the golden surface of Cheekwood's vase. Tiffany achieved his hallmark iridescent surfaces through a specific lustering technique that involved dissolving metallic oxides in the molten glass, creating a crackled surface of tiny, light-refracting lines. By 1894 Tiffany seemed to have perfected the technique for making his distinctive and splendid wares and invented the term favrile, probably inspired by the Old English word for handmade, to distinguish the pieces from other art-glass objects.

The trumpet vase seen here is certainly a testament to the cutting-edge experiments in glass and fine craftsmanship that Tiffany used to produce such innovative and aesthetically beautiful objects. Indeed, the continued popularity and admiration for Tiffany wares today validates the artist's declaration that "handicraft which possesses beauty and originality is independent of passing fashion."

LOUIS COMFORT TIFFANY
Self Portrait, 1872.
NATIONAL ACADEMY OF DESIGN, NEW YORK.

Trumpet Vase, c. 1899–1928, glass, Gift of Allen O. and Elizabeth C. Mason, 1995.15.20

DETAIL: STUART DAVIS (AMERICAN, 1894-1964) *Untitled*, 1964, FROM THE *Ten Works by Ten Painters* PORTFOLIO, ANONYMOUS GIFT, 1965.3.1

In art economy is always beauty.

Henry James, Prefaces 1907-1909

FRANK DUVENECK (AMERICAN, 1848–1919), *Portrait of John Henry Twachtman*, N.D., OIL ON CANVAS, GIFT OF MR. AND MRS. WALTER KNESTRICK, 1985.29.3 DUVENECK WAS TWACHTMAN'S FIRST TEACHER, AND HE ENCOURAGED HIM TO PAINT IN A DARK BROWN PALETTE. A TRIP TO PARIS IN THE MID-1880S EXPOSED TWACHTMAN TO IMPRESSIONISM AND SUBSEQUENTLY LIGHTENED HIS PALETTE, BUT HIS FRIENDSHIP WITH THE MUNICH-STYLE ARTIST REMAINED STRONG THROUGHOUT HIS LIFETIME.

JOHN HENRY TWACHTMAN (AMERICAN, 1853–1902), *Untitled (landscape)*, N.D., OIL ON PANEL, GIFT OF MR. ROBERT P. COGGINS, 1983.1 TWACHTMAN'S FASCINATION WITH THE GREENWICH FARM STRETCHED OVER THE FULL THIRTEEN YEARS OF OWNERSHIP. THIS PAINTING OF A POOL RESEMBLES THE FARM'S HEMLOCK POOL THAT TWACHTMAN PAINTED MANY TIMES.

PHOTOGRAPH OF JOHN HENRY TWACHTMAN, c. 1900. Photographed by Gertrude Kasebier. Photographs of Artists Collection I. Archives of American Art. Smithsonian Institution.

And I was green and carefree, famous among the barns
About the happy yard and singing as the farm was home,
In the sun that is young once only,
Time let me play and be
Golden in the mercy of his means…
–DYLAN THOMAS, FERN HILL

In this pastel John Henry Twachtman lovingly depicts his Connecticut farm as if it were a half-remembered dream. Bare brown paper peeks out from behind the scumbled drawing, a quick impression of the scene produced on site. Twachtman bought the property on Round Hill Road, two miles beyond Greenwich, in 1890 with funds generated from successful art sales of the previous year. He and his family spent thirteen years adapting the house and its seventeen acres. During that time, Twachtman painted numerous renditions of the front and back of the house, as well as the brook, the pool, and the gardens. Cheekwood's pastel portrays the front of the house and nearby barn from a low vantage near the base of Round Hill. Below left is a suggestion of a pond.

The artist's orchard appears as two groups of trees to the left and right of center, reversing the line of the hillside. The meager number and disarray of the trees tell us that the orchard is not intensely cultivated or especially productive. A 1905 article in *Country Life* describes the Twachtman farm as "one of the few blessed country places where nothing is done of a useful rural sort." We know from his work that the garden produced almost no vegetables and was filled mostly with flowers. Twachtman was a romantic whose real interest lay in recreating on canvas or paper the comfort and joy that he found in Greenwich.

Twachtman drew directly on his paper with pastels, rarely smudging them to mix the colors. His brown paper, a shade he favored, added depth to the bright purples and greens of the pastel medium. He used three shades of green to delineate different areas of the hill: an olive shade dominates, but a lighter spring green covers the hill's top round, suggesting a cleared meadow of new grass; occasionally, a forest green depicts a dark thicket. Purple creates a cool area, denoting a change in gradient. The remainder of the scene is composed of a blue-gray and the occasional dark line.

The pastel medium underwent a revival in the 1880s, under the influence of James Abbott McNeil Whistler and Edgar Degas, who were then working in France. Twachtman's technique of applying the pastel directly onto colored paper, allowing areas of the paper to show through, recalls the work of Whistler. Twachtman exhibited with the Society of Painters in Pastel in 1888 and at the Wunderlich Gallery in 1891 and 1893. Today, over one hundred years after those showings, Twachtman's garden scenes seem fresh and immediate.

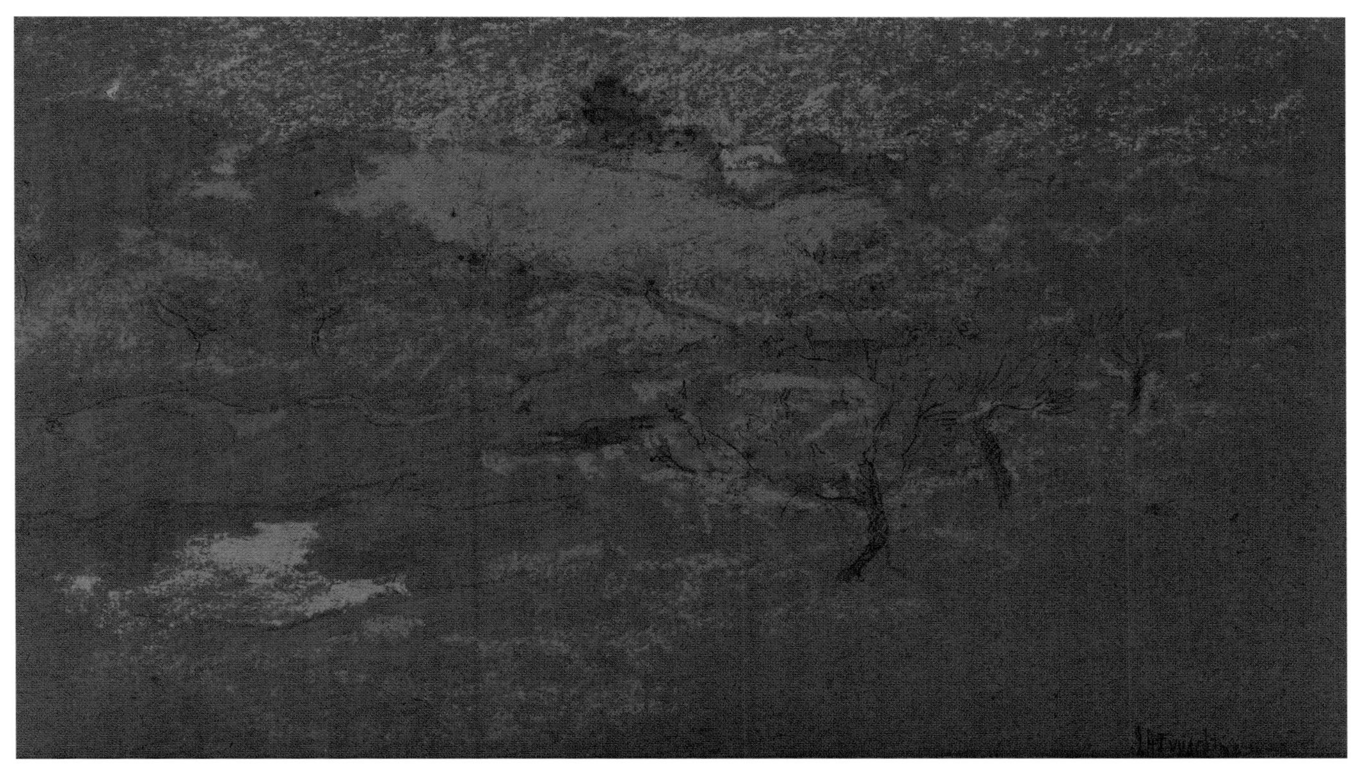

Orchard, c. 1889, pastel and pencil, Museum Purchase through the bequest of Anita Bevill McMichael Stallworth, 1988.14.3

Via Garibaldi, 1898–99, WATERCOLOR, MUSEUM PURCHASE THROUGH THE BEQUEST OF ANITA BEVILL McMICHAEL STALLWORTH, 1995.4

MAURICE PRENDERGAST (AMERICAN, 1859–1924)

This sunny depiction of vacationers and residents strolling along a Venetian avenue was painted by the forty-year old Maurice Prendergast during his third trip to Europe. A first trip, when the young artist worked a cattle boat to England, left little impression on the artist's work. During his second, more influencing, trip, taken seven years prior to this watercolor, Prendergast began to paint outdoors in the cafes and parks of urban Paris. His subjects recall the women in fellow-Bostonian Childe Hassam's Parisian scenes of a few years earlier and in the magazine illustrations of James A. M. Whistler. This second trip was equally important to Prendergast for the contacts he made with other artists at the Chat Blanc cafe in Montparness, particularly James Wilson Morrice, a Canadian painter with similar sensibilities. Morrice was possibly Prendergast's connection to Robert Henri, who, ten years later, invited Prendergast to exhibit with the Eight, who in 1908 at the MacBeth Gallery in New York, were among the first American artists to hold an independent exhibit of their works.

With financial assistance from his patrons, Prendergast returned to Europe in 1898. This time his focus was Italy: the winter in Rome, side trips to the hill towns and to the south, and then Venice, where he spent the last half of his visit. Working almost exclusively in watercolors, Prendergast painted the picturesque bridges, canals, and palazzos of Venice. Populating these images are the women who first appeared in the Parisian scenes, clutching brightly colored parasols or the hands of wandering children. They are a mixture of chatting fashionable ladies and working-class subjects, perhaps the children's nannies. While many of the Parisian scenes were painted from a high vantage point, so that the crowd becomes a mosaic of dabs of color, in *Via Garibaldi* the vantage is closer so that the viewer seems a part of the scene, as the caregiver turns to meet our gaze. Two lines of trees that recede into the background and create the illusion of depth flank the avenue, named for the Italian nationalist revolutionary Giuseppe Garibaldi (1807–1882). The sun is coming from the right, creating deep shadows on the right flank of trees that Prendergast painted with a deep French blue, a technique he would certainly have seen in France in the work of Impressionists such as Andre Derain. *Via Garibaldi* leads into the Public Gardens, where the Venice Biennale is held on alternate years. The overhead banners may relate to the country pavilions of the Biennale, which would have taken place between June and September of 1899, when Prendergast was in residence. The bright spots of color enlivened his scenes and were well suited in shape to his paint application, which involved daubs of color laid on the paper in a mosaic-like pattern, much like the pointillist technique of Paul Signac.

Prendergast returned to Boston in late 1899. *Via Garibaldi* was exhibited the following year at the Art Institute of Chicago and at the MacBeth Gallery in New York. Prendergast would return to Italy in 1911, his fourth trip. By then his technique would have changed, his daubs of color lengthening into strong square brush strokes to emphasize the surface of the painting over the subject, transforming his fashionable ladies into ghostly figures in a motionless frieze.

MAURICE PRENDERGAST (AMERICAN, 1859–1924), *Mountain Landscape,* N.D., WATERCOLOR, PASTEL AND PENCIL, GIFT OF MR. AND MRS. WALTER KNESTRICK, 1985.29.10 AFTER 1903 PRENDERGAST MOVED AWAY FROM THE POINTILLIST TECHNIQUE, LENGTHENING HIS WATERCOLOR BRUSH STROKES.

PHOTOGRAPH OF MAURICE B. PRENDERGAST, 1913. PHOTOGRAPHED BY GERTRUDE KASEBIER. PHOTOGRAPHS OF ARTISTS COLLECTION I. ARCHIVES OF AMERICAN ART. SMITHSONIAN INSTITUTION.

EVERETT SHINN (AMERICAN, 1876–1953), *Is He Home?*, 1903, PASTEL AND PENCIL, GIFT OF MR. AND MRS. WALTER KNESTRICK, 1981.26.13 THEATER SUBJECTS WOULD REPLACE SHINN'S URBAN SCENES AFTER 1907.

EVERETT SHINN (AMERICAN, 1876–1953), *Girl Sleeping*, N.D., CONTE CRAYON, GIFT OF DR. AND MRS. BENJAMIN H. CALDWELL, JR., 1976.4.45 THIS SUBJECT MAY BE A BEHIND-THE-SCENES VIEW OF THE THEATER.

EVERETT SHINN (AMERICAN, 1876–1953), *Bridal Path, Central Park*, N.D., CONTE CRAYON AND PASTEL, MUSEUM PURCHASE WITH FUNDS FROM THE WALTER SHARP MEMORIAL FUND, 1972.10.16 SHINN'S PREFERRED MEDIUM WAS PASTEL, WHICH ALLOWED HIM TO SKETCH A SCENE QUICKLY AND TO CAPTURE THE COLORFUL NATURE OF HIS SUBJECTS.

PHOTOGRAPH OF EVERETT SHINN. PHOTOGRAPHS OF ARTISTS COLLECTION I. ARCHIVES OF AMERICAN ART. SMITHSONIAN INSTITUTION.

EVERETT SHINN (AMERICAN, 1876–1953)

One of the most common catastrophes in turn-of-the-century American cities was destruction by fire. A review of any major newspaper from the period is likely to yield a report covering a conflagration in Chicago, in St. Louis, or, as here, in New York City. Several reasons accounted for the frequency of New York's major fires: industrial development caused intense urban congestion; fire codes were not up to modern-day standards (New York's famous Triangle Shirtwaist Company fire of 1910 would eventually lead to fire-code reform); and construction relied mostly on wood, keeping the city's local fire department, a volunteer organization until after the Civil War, very busy.

As a newspaper illustrator for New York's *World*, *Journal*, and *Herald*, Everett Shinn experienced the raging fires of the city firsthand. Newspapers like the *World*, owned by Joseph Pulitzer, were well known for their sensational stories that appealed to immigrants' thirst for news and entertainment from the street. Shinn learned to sketch quickly to replicate the spontaneous, combustible moment, providing the papers who employed him with firsthand illustrations of dramatic scenes.

Fire on Twenty-Fourth Street, like most of Shinn's early drawings, presents its subject in a theatrical fashion, the deep shadows of the adjacent structures playing off against the backlit fire and brilliant snow. Even the format of the drawing is stage-like: a foreground row of onlookers acting as proscenium, a middle ground for the firefighters' bustling activity, and the skyscrapers acting as background. But by 1907 Everett Shinn had quit newspaper work. His art career was up and running, with several one-person exhibits in Paris, Philadelphia, and New York to his credit. While urban scenes like this fire occasionally attracted the artist, Shinn had found a new subject of interest. The architect Stanford White, a good friend of Shinn's, introduced him to David Belasco, who commissioned Shinn to paint murals for Belasco's Stuyvesant Theater in 1907. Shinn had already become obsessed with theatrical culture, and his pastels after this date almost exclusively treat theater subjects.

The four engines seen in this pastel are self-propelled steamers similar to models made by the LaFrance Fire Engine Company, the American Fire Engine Company, and the Amoskeag Company, although manufacture of hand-pumpers continued in the United States until 1910. The sparks hovering over the engines come from the fires beneath the engines' boilers, generating steam to pump the water. In the middle ground is a wheel-turned hook-and-ladder truck, a hand-cranked device that could not reach above the fourth floor. Because the steamers only accommodated three passengers, other firemen had to run alongside the steamers. The fire chief would have arrived in the horse-drawn buggy seen at the left. Even today, a fire chief's official car is referred to as "the buggy." The night scene is no theatrical construct: most fires occurred at night when factories were deserted and fires had a chance to spread. Whether residential or industrial, fires were most common in the winter, sparked by fireplaces and lanterns.

Fire on Twenty-Fourth Street, 1907, PASTEL ON PAPER, GIFT OF THE 1995 COLLECTORS' GROUP WITH MATCHING FUNDS THROUGH THE BEQUEST OF ANITA BEVILL MCMICHAEL STALLWORTH, 1995.7

Landscape in Waterford, Connecticut, 1917, PASTEL, MUSEUM PURCHASE THROUGH THE BEQUEST OF ANITA BEVILL MCMICHAEL
STALLWORTH, 1998.14.1

WILLARD METCALF (AMERICAN, 1858–1925)

Willard Metcalf spent the summers between 1915 and 1919 in Waterford, a small town in southeastern Connecticut at the mouth of the Niantic River on the Long Island Sound. Metcalf and his second wife, the former Henriette A. McCrea, whom he married in 1911, vacationed each summer with their two children, Rosalind and Addison, at the same colonial house on Jordan's Cove. The artist created many images of Waterford and of his family during those summers, including this pastel of an inlet on the Niantic. A wooden bridge spans the center of the composition, framed by indigenous poplar trees growing on the nearby shore. The framing device, which Metcalf picked up early in his studies, focuses the viewer's eye on the most important part of the painting, the bridge. Metcalf's student sketchbook from the School of the Fine Arts in Boston, which he attended from 1876 to 1879, contains a similar image but with a gateway as a frame. Another popular device Metcalf uses is the receding waterway that forms a jagged diagonal across the Waterford picture plane to suggest depth.

The five summers during World War I that Metcalf spent on the New England coast provided ample subjects for his work and allowed him to supplement his income by teaching. In 1917 the European tenor Luciano Muratore studied with Metcalf, along with Muratore's wife, Lina Cavalieri, also an opera singer, and Cavalieri's accompanist, M. Pintelli. Pintelli was so taken by Metcalf's paintings that he wrote a nocturne based on the artist's *A Summer Night* (1914). The Metcalfs loved the area, staying there in 1918 even when an influenza epidemic forced them, as Henriette noted, to survive by "wearing masks and living on whiskey and castor oil." When the Jordan's Cove house was put on the market in 1919, the Metcalfs considered buying but rented a nearby house instead and did not return to Waterford again.

Metcalf is best known for these New England winter scenes, some of which were painted in Cornish, New Hampshire, and in Maine. He had spent 1903 alone in Maine, recovering from a disastrous first marriage. There, he experimented with a looser brush stroke and a lighter palette. Metcalf described 1903 as his "Renaissance," for it was during this period of retreat that he developed his own personal style of Impressionism, undoubtedly influenced by the work of his friend and colleague John H. Twachtman.

Twachtman, along with William Merritt Chase and J. Alden Weir, was a leader of the American Impressionists, a group of artists who adapted the brush stroke, color, and subjects of the European Impressionists. Metcalf, Twachtman, Chase, and Weir had caused a stir in 1897 when they and six like-minded artists resigned in protest from the conservative Society of American Artists for refusing to hold a small exhibit of the group's Impressionist works. The Ten, as they became known, found a private gallery, the Durand-Ruel Gallery at Thirty-Sixth Street and Fifth Avenue in New York, to hold their exhibit, which was so well received by the public that it established the reputations of several of the group. They continued to show annually until Julian Alden Weir, whose friendship had held the group together, died in 1919.

WALTER GRIFFIN (AMERICAN, 1861–1935), *Scene in Norway,* 1910, OIL ON BOARD, GIFT OF DR. AND MRS. BENJAMIN H. CALDWELL, JR., 1976.5.1 WALTER GRIFFIN, ALONG WITH WEIR AND CHILDE HASSAM, TRANSFORMED THE ART COLONY OF OLD LYME FROM THE BARBIZON SCHOOL THAT HENRY WARD RANGER HAD ENVISIONED TO A CENTER FOR IMPRESSIONISM. IT WAS AT OLD LYME THAT GRIFFIN EXPLORED THE POINTILLIST STYLE FOUND IN *SCENE IN NORWAY.*

HENRY WARD RANGER (AMERICAN, 1858–1916), *Untitled,* 1908, OIL ON CANVAS, GIFT OF THE BERNAL FOUNDATION IN MEMORY OF BERNARD WERTHAN, 1984.2

PHOTOGRAPH OF WILLARD METCALF, c. 1920. PHOTOGRAPHED BY NICKOLAS MURRAY. PHOTOGRAPHS OF ARTISTS COLLECTION I. ARCHIVES OF AMERICAN ART. SMITHSONIAN INSTITUTION.

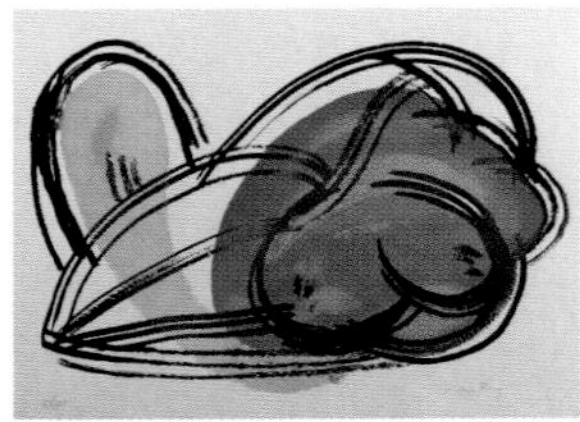

MAN RAY (AMERICAN, 1890–1976), *Nudo,* 1964, LITHOGRAPH, MUSEUM PURCHASE THROUGH THE BEQUEST OF ANITA BEVILL MCMICHAEL STALLWORTH, 1992.11

PHOTOGRAPH OF JOHN MARIN, C. 1950. PHOTOGRAPHS OF ARTISTS COLLECTION II. ARCHIVES OF AMERICAN ART. SMITHSONIAN INSTITUTION.

JOHN MARIN (AMERICAN, 1870–1953)

John Marin worked as an architect before studying art at the Pennsylvania Academy of the Fine Arts and at the Art Students League. He then spent five years in Europe, where he was influenced not by the French Postimpressionists popular by then, but by the Impressionists James McNeil Whistler, Paul Signac, and Pierre Bonnard. When he returned to the United States in 1910, he was introduced to Alfred Stieglitz and the 291 Gallery, where Marin experienced his first serious exposure to the work of Paul Cezanne, Pablo Picasso, and Georges Bracque. During the next three years, Marin's sole subject matter was New York City. For Marin, the city was alive with movement. By 1912 he developed a mature style in a series of watercolors of the city, using forms from the environment to express emotion.

In 1913, Marin spent his first summer in Maine and turned to painting landscapes. The modernist landscape painters Georgia O'Keeffe, Arthur Dove, and Charles Burchfield, whom Marin knew from the 291 Gallery, wanted not only to capture the object in nature but also to grasp the spirit of the object and to express their own subjective responses. To these artists, the process of placing pigment on the canvas was as important as the arrangement of their compositions. While Marin embraced these principles, his art is more about interacting with than intellectualizing nature.

Marin experimented with true abstraction for the first and only time in 1917. Two texts seem to have been instrumental in this decision: a translated excerpt of Wassily Kandinsky's 1912 essay "Concerning the Spiritual in Art" published in *Camera Work*, and Arthur Wesley Dow's *Abstraction in Art*, published in 1917. Both works present form and color as critical compositional elements. Friend and photographer Paul Strand wrote in an essay for a 1921 exhibition of Marin's work that Marin may have been struggling to overcome the influence of Whistler and Chinese landscape painting and to move directly to the environment and animate the forces behind it.

This 1917 watercolor is an example of Marin's experimentation with abstraction. These precise shapes and the controlled color application show none of Marin's earlier use of brush strokes and pigment to imply movement; moreover, the intellectualization of composition is in sharp contrast to his more fluid works. An inverted triangular arrangement provides the framework for the major compositional elements. Within the triangle, the discernible forms of a square and oval are contrasted with an amorphous five-pronged figure that leaves viewers to respond in their own way to Marin's curious figural subject.

Abstraction, 1917, WATERCOLOR, GIFT OF THE 1990 COLLECTORS' GROUP WITH MATCHING FUNDS THROUGH THE BEQUEST OF ANITA BEVILL MCMICHAEL STALLWORTH, 1990.6.2

Kathleen Millay, 1925, CRAYON AND METAL POINT ON PAPER, MUSEUM PURCHASE THROUGH THE BEQUEST OF ANITA BEVILL McMICHAEL STALLWORTH, 1989.8.1

JOSEPH STELLA (AMERICAN, B. ITALY, 1877–1946)

–Edna St. Vincent Millay, "To Kathleen"

Joseph Stella enjoyed combining traditional art techniques with the bold, rebellious ideals of modern art. In the portrait of Kathleen Millay, Stella revived the Renaissance technique of silver point, the use of a silver rod to produce delicate, gray lines. By employing the flattened space found in his modernistic works, Stella created a sensual portrait of a vivacious, spirited woman. Just as the towering structure in his most famous painting, *The Brooklyn Bridge*, appears as a metaphor for the modern, industrial age, Kathleen symbolizes the growing independence of women in the 1920s. Kathleen Millay was the youngest sister of the famous poet, author, and playwright Edna St. Vincent Millay. Kathleen followed in Edna's footsteps, writing several novels and collections of poetry. Although she did not achieve the literary acclaim of Edna, she was widely noted for her classic, dark-haired, Irish beauty and her even-tempered but independent personality. Stella depicted the strength and willfulness of her character through her forceful, frontal pose and aggressive, confrontational stare. By placing Kathleen, loosely wrapped in a kimono-like robe, in a context of flattened space and Japanese print pattern, Stella also further accentuated and transmitted the exotic quality of Kathleen's personality.

Joseph Stella, an immigrant from a middle-class Italian family, came to New York when he was eighteen years old. Emulating the medical-career path of an older brother, who also immigrated to the United States, Stella studied medicine and pharmacology in New York. Soon, however, Stella's natural talent for draftsmanship inspired him to enroll in art school. He received his art education in the academic manner, initially at the Art Students League and, finally, at the New York School of Art, founded and headed by William Merritt Chase, one of America's most famous artists and art teachers. Studying Chase, Stella mastered Chase's bravura brush stroke and sense of light and shade, receiving high praise from Chase himself.

During a trip to his homeland in 1909, Stella discovered the Italian Futurists, Cubism, and other avant-garde movements. Influenced by the modular, linear character of these styles, a radical change occurred in Stella's aesthetic as he seemed to break instantly and completely from his academic education. He dropped the imitative, Old Master appearance of his work and its dark palette, replacing them with flattened space, geometrical forms, and bold colors. Stella quickly stepped into the spotlight, forging the path of modernist art in America. His Futurist-inspired works embraced the power of industry in an almost spiritual manner. Having become by the early 1920s one of the most financially successful modern artists, Stella, as seen in *Kathleen Millay*, turned back to the Old Masters and the Renaissance, combining that heritage with the modern approach he brought to America.

JOSEPH STELLA (AMERICAN, B. ITALY, 1877–1946), *Flowers with Dogwood, n.d.* SILVER POINT AND COLOR PENCILS ON PAPER. GIFT OF MR. SERGIO STELLA 1983.4 INSPIRED BY THE WORKS OF FOURTEENTH- AND FIFTEENTH-CENTURY FLEMISH PAINTERS, STELLA BASED MANY OF HIS PAINTINGS ON FLORAL MOTIFS. *FLOWERS WITH DOGWOOD* DEMONSTRATES HIS CAREFUL STUDY OF RENDERING PLANT LIFE.

PHOTOGRAPH OF JOSEPH STELLA, C. 1940. PHOTOGRAPHS OF ARTISTS COLLECTION I. ARCHIVES OF AMERICAN ART. SMITHSONIAN INSTITUTION.

COMPARISONS:

CHARLES BURCHFIELD (AMERICAN, 1893-1967), *Gothic House,* 1920, WATERCOLOR, ACQUISITIONS DINNER PURCHASE IN MEMORY OF DAVID STEINE WITH FUNDS PROVIDED BY MR. AND MRS. GEORGE CLARK, THE EXCHANGE CLUB CHARITIES, MR. AND MRS. JACK C. MASSEY, MR. AND MRS. JOHN STAMPS AND MR. AND MRS. ALBERT WERTHAN. 1976.10.7

CHARLES BURCHFIELD (AMERICAN, 1893-1967), *Pigeons Flying,* N.D., WATERCOLOR AND PENCIL, GIFT OF MR. AND MRS. WALTER KNESTRICK, 1986.16.6

PHOTOGRAPH OF CHARLES E. BURCHFIELD. PHOTOGRAPHS OF ARTISTS COLLECTION I. ARCHIVES OF AMERICAN ART. SMITHSONIAN INSTITUTION.

An artist must paint, not what he sees in Nature, but what is there. To do so he must invent symbols, which, if properly used, make his work seem even more real than what is in front of him. He does not try to by-pass Nature; his work is superior to Nature's surface appearances, but not to its basic laws.
—CHARLES BURCHFIELD

Charles Burchfield, whether depicting urban scenes, houses, or landscapes, often personified his subject matter. Trees often take on dispositions of their own. Some stand in full, leafy, bloom, bustling with life, and others cower, barren, withered, or stooped. In *The Dead Trees,* two stark, lifeless trees stand out against a lush background of rolling, fertile hills. One tree lies on the ground stretching across the picture plane like a fallen soldier, while the other, still rooted to the ground, leans to the left in decay. Both are depicted in a transparent manner as they fade and disintegrate into the soil.

Like much of Burchfield's work, *The Dead Trees* draws on the attitudes and theories of the earlier Hudson River School. Those artists shared a sense of awe for the land and an almost religious, spiritual connection with nature. The writings of Ralph Waldo Emerson, a transcendentalist who believed that man's potential can be fulfilled only through close contact with the beauty, truth, and goodness found in nature, and John Muir, a naturalist and nature conservationist, inspired Burchfield's cryptic, mystical scenes of nature. Because traditional painting often contained symbols to promote a deeper meaning, Burchfield developed his own artistic language using the stylized forms and decorative lines of Art Nouveau to describe human experience in terms of nature. Burchfield often used stark, leafless trees, either solitary or in groups, to represent the frailty of human life.

Cheekwood's permanent collection contains two other works by Burchfield. He painted *Pigeons Flying* at the beginning of his career, when his work was filled with mysterious, morose landscapes derived from his dreams and childhood memories. It recalls painter Robert Henri's statement in his book *The Art Spirit:* "Reveal the spirit you have about the thing, not the materials you are going to paint. . . . Rather paint the flying spirit of the bird than its feathers." Burchfield also sought to express vitality in the scenes he depicted rather than to copy the subject before him. *Pigeons Flying* seems eerie, empty, and desolate and would be lifeless without the birds tracing the sky. However, to Burchfield, birds represented freedom and religious spirituality.

Gothic House exemplifies a transition in the 1920s from natural subjects, as in *The Dead Trees,* to realistic urban scenes. Sherwood Anderson, among other American realist writers, led Burchfield to reevaluate his pictorial direction. Anderson's 1919 book, *Winesburg, Ohio,* presents a collage of moments in a small Northern town where residents, although sharing a community, remain secluded from one another and stifled in their own situations and lives. Burchfield likewise sought to depict visually the feelings of isolation and desolation in urban and rural life during the American industrial age. As in his early landscapes, houses took on animated personalities and secrets of their own. Twenty-two years later, Burchfield would reconcile his realistic manner with the earlier mysterious, dream-like landscapes in the final phase of his career.

The Dead Trees, N.D., WATERCOLOR, GIFT OF MR. AND MRS. WALTER KNESTRICK, 1981.26.1

Mrs. Ramsey, Gatlinburg, Tennessee, 1933, GELATIN SILVERPRINT, GIFT OF THE ARTIST, 1984.24.93

LOUISE DAHL-WOLFE (AMERICAN, 1895–1989)

Louise Dahl-Wolfe became one of the best-known fashion and portrait photographers from the Golden Age of fashion photography. Her pioneering use of color, bold graphic backgrounds, and art-historical borrowings transformed the look of fashion photography. Dahl-Wolfe documented and, in her own way, created *haute couture* for the innovative *Harper's Bazaar* from 1936 to 1958. It became the number one fashion magazine in America due to the now-famous creative team of Carmel Snow, editor-in-chief; Diana Vreeland, fashion editor; Alexey Brodovitch, art director; and Dahl-Wolfe. Dahl-Wolfe had complete artistic control of her work, and her perfectionism remains legendary.

Dahl-Wolfe toppled the European standard of frozen glamour with an energetic, natural vision of the fashionable woman. In a world dominated by stiff, lifelessly posed models, Dahl-Wolfe photographed models in a way that emphasized elegance and natural grace. One of the first to shoot models at exotic outdoor locations, Dahl-Wolfe utilized such locations as the Yucatan, Paris, Rio, and the Caribbean and treated the background and landscape as integral to the photographic look and concept. She worked at *Harper's Bazaar* for twenty-two years and later for *Vogue* and *Sports Illustrated*. Her inventiveness did not stop with fashion photography; she also excelled in the genre of portraits, from the intensely moving studies of the Depression-era women from the Tennessee hills to the most celebrated personalities of this century.

In November 1933 *Vanity Fair* published Louise Dahl-Wolfe's photograph of an East Tennessee woman taken during the Depression. Dahl-Wolfe was recognized overnight as a major talent. Originally titled *Tennessee Mountain Woman*, the photograph exhibits Dahl-Wolfe's extraordinary talent in portraiture and composition. In a manner similar to Matisse, Dahl-Wolfe composed her background with many individual elements that accentuate the sitter. In *Mrs. Ramsey*, Dahl-Wolfe's compositional strengths reflect carefully measured relationships of light, shadow, pattern, and form. Foreshadowing her career photographing models, Dahl-Wolfe composed the photograph with signifiers indicating the subject's identity and milieu. The uneven, peeling paint of the wallboards contrasts with the rhythmic patterning of the checkerboard tablecloth; the lamp, often a symbol for truth in art history, here reflects the lack of electricity in the pre-TVA era in the Tennessee hills. Mrs. Ramsey's head and folded arms recreate the triangular pose used in Renaissance portraits such as Leonardo's *Mona Lisa*. Her big, round hat creates something of a dark halo around Mrs. Ramsey. Dahl-Wolfe's portraits, regardless of the sitter, offer a sense of the psychological inner person that has become a hallmark of all her portraiture.

PHOTOGRAPH OF
LOUISE DAHL-WOLFE.
©1989 CENTER FOR CREATIVE PHOTOGRAPHY,
ARIZONA BOARD OF REGENTS.

works on paper

YASUMASA MORIMURA (JAPANESE, B. 1951)
Ambiguous Beauty/Aimai-No-Bi, N.D.,
PAPER, FABRIC, AND PLASTIC,
GIFT OF THE PETER NORTON FAMILY, 1995.11

PHOTOGRAPH OF REGINALD MARSH
PHOTOGRAPHS OF ARTISTS COLLECTION II.
ARCHIVES OF AMERICAN ART.
SMITHSONIAN INSTITUTION.

REGINALD MARSH (AMERICAN, B. FRANCE 1898–1954)

With its sprawling figures, *Coney Island* portrays reunited couples writhing in joyful celebration following World War II. Marsh heightened this passion by portraying an environment full of emotional conflict, a scene at once joyous and lewd, festive and aggressive. *Coney Island* portrays the chaos of humanity controlled by the order of the artist's hand. This passionate debauchery is not rendered in a cavalier manner but is encased in a neatly stratified, circular, and carefully cropped composition. The kinetic design of the image adds to the sexually charged revelry and reflects Marsh's desire to express motion in his paintings. *Coney Island* also represents a shift in Marsh's priorities, giving familiar subject matter a permanent back seat to the more formal aspects of his painting, namely, light, color, composition, and brushwork.

For Marsh, Coney Island was the ideal setting for figures in motion, providing Marsh with what Bernard Danenberg describes as "crowds of people in all directions, in all positions, without clothing, moving—like the great compositions of Michelangelo and Rubens." Marsh, who decided to become a professional artist after copying Rubens and Delacroix in Paris for six months (1925–1926), also studied human anatomy at two New York medical colleges. Like da Vinci and Michelangelo before him, he mastered the structure of the human body by dissecting cadavers. Very much alive and somewhat stylized, however, the bodies in *Coney Island* become a visual hyperbole for life itself—carpe-diem in the flesh.

The shoulder-to-shoulder crowd of *Coney Island* was a staple of Marsh's subject matter during his career. Also recurring in his work were images of hyped-up human energy from New York street life, the burlesque, and the Bowery. Incorporated in these themes are subplots involving what critic and friend Lloyd Goodrich referred to as "the magnetic power of the female body" and "the public pursuit of pleasure." *Coney Island*—with its men attending to buxom women in suggestive poses—stands as a superb example of Marsh's fascination with these characteristics of New York life.

During a thirty-year career of recording life in the city, Marsh experimented with a variety of media, struggling to find the one most appropriate to his style and subjects. It was with the discovery of egg tempera in the late twenties that he began to create the large and powerful compositions that established his reputation as a painter. Marsh would, as with *Coney Island*, periodically return to watercolor in combination with Chinese ink. These works maintained the spirit of Marsh's earlier paintings yet expanded his new-found passion for painting as process. The result is a body of work consisting of fantastical, almost phantasmagoric, figures.

On the surface, the translucence of Marsh's beach crowd in *Coney Island* might be attributed to the water-based media and to his emphasis on the formal aspects of painting. This literal fading away of the subjects in Marsh's work, however, is also a metaphor for his feeling of loss as he observed the changing cultural landscape of New York—a melancholy yearning for a passing era, which led him to muse late in life, "Everything I've loved is disappearing. They've torn down the El; the burlesque is gone, I hardly recognize Coney Island anymore."

Coney Island, 1945, Chinese ink and watercolor on paper, Gift of the 1991 Collectors' Group with matching funds through the bequest of Anita Bevill McMichael Stallworth, 1991.3

STUDY FOR *The Boy,* 1949, watercolor and ink, Gift of Mr. and Mrs. John A. Hill, 1991.10.1

THOMAS HART BENTON (AMERICAN, 1889–1975)

The meanings [of the images] are, of course, indeterminate, suggested rather than precisely defined, and open to free interpretation, as I believe they should be. In the end, the meanings of the pictures must be found by those who view them.

—Thomas Hart Benton

In *The Boy*, telephone polls along a country road symbolize technology's encroachment into rural areas. A young man waving good-bye to his parents abandons his agrarian upbringing for the promise of the industrial city. Benton usually sketched his ideas for new paintings in watercolor and ink. Unlike the solid, sculpted appearance of his paintings and murals, Benton constructed preliminary studies with bright, flat colors and dark, heavy outlines. By portraying scenes of ordinary American life in the Midwest, Thomas Hart Benton gained popularity at a time when abstraction and modernistic approaches were beginning to dominate the art scene.

With the rise of modernist art theories, art circles stirred with new aesthetic ideas, clashing opinions, and competitive spirits in the early twentieth century. Artists who found the academic tradition formulaic, obsolete, and unsatisfying looked for new modes of expression in color, presentation, and subject matter. Like many American artists, Benton crossed the Atlantic to the Académie Julian in Paris, then one of the foremost art schools in the world. During his three years there, he refined his skills in draftsmanship and painting techniques. Not limiting himself to the study of Renaissance and Old Master paintings, Benton grew interested in Postimpressionist artists, such as Paul Gaugin and Paul Cezanne, for their formal innovations and studied new aesthetic theories, such as Cubism and Fauvism. After returning to America, he experimented extensively with abstraction as a participant in American Synchronism, an art movement known for its intense color and geometric shapes. Eventually, however, Benton found modernism empty and insufficient for his artistic needs.

Born into a politically active Missouri family (his father and great uncle were both outspoken U.S. Senators), Benton carried on family tradition by supporting the Midwestern interests in opposition to the Eastern. Although Benton's work does not promote any social causes, he elevated Midwestern subject matter, whether agrarian or industrial, urban or rural, as valid subject matter for high art. Controversial throughout his career, Benton was heavily criticized by some for his subjects and style but was just as enthusiastically praised by others. He anchored his work in the lives of common Americans and wanted his paintings to appeal to the "man on the street," not to the art critics in New York. Without abandoning his academic training, Benton developed a purely American style that combined simple, almost monochromatic, color palettes with Renaissance-like sculptural forms and elongated, exaggerated proportions derived from the paintings of El Greco.

COMPARISON:

THOMAS HART BENTON (AMERICAN, 1889–1975), *Plowing It Under*, 1934, LITHOGRAPH, GIFT OF MRS. ROBERT B. CARTWRIGHT, 1973.9.5 IN THE SPRING OF 1933, THE U.S. GOVERNMENT PASSED FRANKLIN D. ROOSEVELT'S AGRICULTURAL ADJUSTMENT ACT IN AN EFFORT TO RAISE COTTON PRICES AND, THEREBY, THE INCOME OF FARMERS DURING THE DEPRESSION. AS CROPS HAD ALREADY BEEN PLANTED BY THE TIME THE BILL WAS IMPLEMENTED, 10.4 MILLION ACRES HAD TO BE "PLOWED UNDER."

PHOTOGRAPH OF THOMAS HART BENTON. PETER A. JULEY & SON COLLECTION. SMITHSONIAN AMERICAN ART MUSEUM.

STUART DAVIS (AMERICAN, 1894–1964)

COMPARISONS:

ROY LICHTENSTEIN (AMERICAN, 1923–1997), *Soda and Sandwich*, 1964, FROM THE *Ten Works by Ten Painters* PORTFOLIO SCREENPRINT ON MYLAR, ANONYMOUS GIFT, 1965.3.4 DAVIS USED SUBJECTS FROM POPULAR CULTURE 30 YEARS EARLIER THAN THE POP ARTISTS IN THE 1960s.

A. C. WEBB, JR. (AMERICAN, 1888–1975) *Empire State Building Under Construction,* N.D., CHARCOAL AND PASTEL, GIFT OF ELLENNA WEBB DOUGLAS, 1984.14.50 DAVIS' WORK IN THE 30's AND 40's WAS HEAVILY INFLUENCED BY THE MASSIVE CONSTRUCTION PROJECTS IN NEW YORK CITY.

PHOTOGRAPH OF STUART DAVIS. PHOTOGRAPHED BY ARNOLD NEWMAN. ARCHIVES OF AMERICAN ART. SMITHSONIAN INSTITUTION.

Born in Philadelphia, Stuart Davis met many working artists at the *Philadelphia Press*, where his father worked as an art editor. In 1910 the family moved to Newark, New Jersey, and Davis soon began studying art with Robert Henri. He frequented Harlem and Newark nightclubs to hear jazz musicians perform. Their freedom of expression and the whole jazz myth influenced greatly Davis's sense of color and form.

Davis exhibited in the 1913 Armory Show, his first exposure to French Postimpressionist painting. The broad generalization of form and the nonimitative use of color—the hallmarks of Paul Gaugin, Vincent Van Gogh, and Henri Matisse—affected Davis as well. He felt that the objective order in their working was lacking in his own. The Armory Show was also Davis's first exposure to Cubism. The Cubists' use of lettering and newsprint in their paintings and collages would be repeated in Davis's work of the early twenties that used advertising and packaging as subjects. While these works are imitative of the early Cubists, their true importance is that of precursor to Pop Art.

In 1928 Davis moved to Paris for a year. While there he began his seminal *Egg Beater* series, his first serious experimentation with abstraction. Upon his return to New York, Davis was both appalled and fascinated by the immensity and chaos of the city that had just experienced a period of massive construction. Davis called Ferdinand Leger "the most American of all painters" for his representation of the man-made urban landscape. Leger's use of De Stijl and Bauhaus principles confirmed Davis's belief that while a painting may be two dimensional, the planes of the composition have different weights and should be balanced. From this, Davis developed a formula of composition that would involve one dominant area of color and form to which all other areas must relate. Davis increasingly used bolder forms and primary colors, often defining areas of composition with black lines.

In 1964, months before his death, Davis completed this print for the *Ten Works by Ten Painters* portfolio published by the Wadsworth Athenaeum. The printed words in the lower left-hand corner and the bold, flat forms in vivid colors recall his earlier Cubist-influenced works. Davis's mature use of rhythmic color and form reflects the continual influence of the jazz myth in a way that is at once jarring and harmonious. The dominant area of the composition encompasses the left third of the print, with the forms and colors used in the rest of the print both mimicking and contrasting the dominant area.

Untitled, 1964, From the *Ten Works by Ten Painters* portfolio, Anonymous Gift, 1965.3.1

DETAIL: EMILE-ANTOINE BOURDELLE (FRENCH, 1861–1929), *Penelope*, 1909, BRONZE. GIFT OF MRS. WALTER SHARP. 1983.5.1

Art!
Who comprehends her?
With whom can one consult concerning
this great goddess?

Ludwig van Beethoven, 1810

William Edmondson was born in Nashville, Tennessee, in 1874 to Orange and Jane Edmondson, former slaves to the Edmondson-Compton families. Edmondson worked for the Nashville, Chattanooga & St. Louis Railroad and also as a racehorse groom, farm hand, and, from 1908 to 1929, as a hospital orderly and fireman at the Woman's Hospital, which later became Baptist Hospital.

When the Depression hit in 1929, he was laid off or quit the hospital. At about this time Edmondson felt he had received a vision from God to carve tombstones. Edmondson said that God told him to "pick up your tools and start to work on a tombstone. I looked up in the sky and right there in the noon daylight He hung a tombstone out for me to make." He began carving tombstones for the two African-American cemeteries in Nashville, Mt. Ararat and Greenwood.

Nearby neighbor Sidney Hirsch—co-leader of the Fugitives, the pioneering literary circle at Vanderbilt University—introduced Edmondson to the Starrs, who in turn introduced Edmondson to Louise Dahl-Wolfe, the well-known fashion photographer of *Harper's Bazaar*. Dahl-Wolfe showed photographs of Edmondson's work to Alfred Barr, the first director of the Museum of Modern Art in New York City. Barr recognized Edmondson's strengths and agreed to show his work in 1937, thus making him the first African-American artist to have a one-man show at MoMA. Barr also included his work in the 1938 international exhibition "300 Hundred Years of American Art" in Paris. After this, however, Edmondson was essentially forgotten by the art world. He died February 7, 1951.

Cheekwood organized the first large-scale retrospective of Edmondson's works in 1964. In 1973 Edmund Fuller wrote the first book on Edmondson, *Visions in Stone: The Sculpture of William Edmondson*. In 1981, the Tennessee State Museum's inaugural exhibition featured a large retrospective on Edmondson and the first scholarly catalog examining his work. But not until the 1982 exhibition at the Corcoran Gallery of Art in Washington, D.C., "Black Folk Art in America, 1930–1980," did Edmondson truly receive widespread recognition. Today he is considered one of the most important self-taught sculptors of the twentieth century.

In this elegant work, Edmondson's neighbors Bess and Joe are transformed into a majestic couple who effortlessly exude grace and dignity. The sculpture evokes simple elegance in a monumental style. Although Edmondson emphasizes the couple's physical differences, he down plays individualistic features in favor of universal appeal. Joe's snap-brim cap and bow tie play off her curly hairdo and lace-collared dress. Her legs peek out from her dress, contrasting greatly with his own removed limb. The couple's stately posture and straight-ahead gaze charge the air around them with quiet calm and simplified splendor. They sit together comfortably, she contentedly with folded arms in her lap, he affectionately comforting her with his arm around her back. They sit as they might on a park bench, casually taking in the world on a Sunday afternoon—the quintessential, majestic couple.

PHOTOGRAPH OF WILLIAM EDMONDSON.
Photographed by Louise Dahl-Wolfe. Collection
Cheekwood Museum of Art, Nashville, TN

Bess and Joe, c. 1935, limestone, Museum Purchase through the bequest of Anita Bevill McMichael Stallworth; and Gift of Salvatore J. Formosa, Sr.; Mrs. Pete A. Formosa, Sr.; Angelo Formosa, Jr.; and Mrs. Rose M. Formosa Bromley in loving memory of Angelo Formosa, Sr., wife Mrs. Katherine St. Charles Formosa, and Pete A. Formosa, Sr., 1993.2.3

Mr. and Mrs. Rembrandt, 1971, wood, fabric and found materials, Gift of Mr. and Mrs. Ervin M. Entrekin and Mr. and Mrs. Walter Knestrick, 1975.9.8

In *Mr. and Mrs. Rembrandt*, one of Red Grooms's first large-scale environmental works, the artist pays homage to the seventeenth-century painter Rembrandt van Rijin (1600–1669) in a portrait that is both whimsical and poignant. The whimsy comes from the artist's technique, which relies on a combination of found objects, bright colors, and flattened perspective that creates a charming caricature of the otherwise high-brow subjects. To clothe his figures, Grooms looted his parents' attic for unusual fabrics and accessories. His folksy technique owes much to the images young Red found in newspaper comics, movies, and the state fair. Grooms was attracted to the homemade character of the brightly colored, otherworldly fair rides.

He adapted the pose of Rembrandt's own painting titled *Saskia van Ulyenburgh* (1641) to portray Rembrandt's wife. As a model for the old master himself, Grooms turned to one of the Dutch artist's later, more elderly self-portraits (Rembrandt painted between fifty and sixty over his lifetime). For the background, Grooms painted the busts, vases, and leather-bound books that undoubtedly decorated Rembrandt's Amsterdam studio. In fact, it was Rembrandt's obsessive acquisition of objects and ornaments that led to his own bankruptcy. Late in his life Rembrandt was forced to sell his home to pay his debts.

The mix of the earlier portrait of Saskia with the later version of Rembrandt reflects what Grooms's assistant, artist Tom Burkhardt, calls Grooms's "fluid sense of history," as seen through the varied lenses of "the Grooms filter." The impossible combination of the aging, gouty Rembrandt with his Springtime bride (who died at the age of 30) adds a bittersweet melancholy to the humorous construction. Grooms again skewed history by placing the old Rembrandt in Grooms's own New York studio, as though the old master were joining a new Pantheon of Pop Art. Grooms even painted an elf in the background, perhaps as a winking gesture to show us that not everything is as it seems.

COMPARISONS:

CHARLES (RED) GROOMS (AMERICAN, B. 1937), *On the Aegean Sea,* 1995, WATERCOLOR, GIFT OF THE 1995 SWAN BALL PATRONS WITH MATCHING FUNDS THROUGH THE BEQUEST OF ANITA BEVILL MCMICHAEL STALLWORTH 1995.6
LIKE REMBRANDT, GROOMS HAS PAINTED SELF-PORTRAITS THROUGHOUT HIS CAREER, SUCH AS CHEEKWOOD'S *On the Aegean.* BOTH MEN'S SELF-IMAGES ARE AMAZINGLY HONEST, EXPOSING THE HUMOR AND PATHOS OF THEIR SUBJECTS.

CHARLES (RED) GROOMS (AMERICAN, B. 1937), *Animation for "Tappy Toes,"* 1969, MIXED MEDIA, COLLAGE, GOUACHE, OIL AND GLITTER, GIFT OF THE NATIONAL ENDOWMENT FOR THE ARTS; THE BERNAL FOUNDATION OF NASHVILLE (WERTHAN FAMILY FOUNDATION); EXCHANGE CLUB CHARITIES; MR. AND MRS. ALVIN G. BEAMAN; MR. AND MRS. MARTIN BROWN; MR. AND MRS. GEORGE CLARK; DR. AND MRS. WILLIAM EWERS; MR. AND MRS. D. W. JOHNSON; MR. AND MRS. DORTCH OLDHAM; DR. AND MRS. ROBERT QUINN; MRS. SARA S. STENGEL; AND DR. AND MRS. CHARLES E. WELLS, 1975.5.3
ALWAYS INTERESTED IN PERFORMANCE ART, GROOMS CREATED THIS DRAWING FOR THE FILM *Tappy Toes,* WHICH USED HIS PICTO-SCULPTO-RAMA, *The City of Chicago,* AS A BACKDROP.

PHOTOGRAPH OF CHARLES (RED) GROOMS, COURTESY OF THE ARTIST.

ENTRY STONE, CHEEKWOOD MANSION
© RICHARD CHEEK

PHOTOGRAPH OF IAN HAMILTON FINLAY
COURTESY OF THE ARTIST.

Poet-sculptor Ian Hamilton Finlay was born in Nassau, Bahamas, in 1925 but soon moved to Scotland where he was reared and presently lives. Originally one of the leaders of concrete poetry, in which the poet uses a word's visual qualities to convey meaning, Finlay eventually distanced himself from that movement to pursue sculpture. He and his wife Sue transformed their humble home in Stonypath, near Edinburgh, into a garden featuring poetry and sculpture in the tradition of eighteenth-century poets. Christened "Little Sparta" after a legal dispute with local tax authorities over its use, it has become one of the world's premier gardens and sculptural sites.

Finlay has been greatly influenced by the goal of the French Revolution to recognize the political concerns and freedoms of the working classes. *The Rights of Man*, formulated during the Revolution and used as a model for individual versus state's rights throughout the world, conceptually informs much of Finlay's sculpture. The work of Louis de Saint-Just, author of the Revolution's rhetoric, has also been appropriated by Finlay and incorporated into his sculptures.

Saint-Just (1767–1794) was known as the "archangel of the French Revolution," a political ideologue viewed as both hero and villain. Fiercely believing in a new society that would recognize the working class, Saint-Just mercilessly persecuted his political opponents during the Reign of Terror. He was guillotined in 1794 along with Robespierre, the architect of the French Revolution. Finlay's work appropriates Saint-Just's epigram to suggest ironically that revolutionary social changes advance the rights and freedoms of the individual working man.

L'ordine del presente e il disordine del *futuro* (the Order of the Present Is the Disorder of the Future). Conceptually, the epigram, written in Italian, portends a morality tale that attempts to predict the future. Finlay orchestrated the epigram into these huge, dramatic stones to suggest the inherent tensions between man, culture, and nature. Physically, these giant stone tablets suggest the ruins of a Roman temple or the fragments from an ancient regime's now-forgotten policy or law.

Both the words and tablets draw into consideration their present context (the surrounding trees, the gardens, the house on the hill). The phrase's twisting, ironic playfulness asks one to consider: Which is the order and which is the disorder? Are the stones, now in ruin, the collapsed order of the yesterday? Or do they signify the chaotic order of today's world?

Perhaps no other artwork on the trail has a firmer connection to the Cheekwood mansion and gardens than Finlay's. Look up the vista toward the house, and there on the hilltop is a cultural symbol of neoclassical order and design. Surrounding you are the woods and gardens of nature. On the hill, authority; in the woods, chaos. Fallen stones from another time beckon you to reconsider your position between the two.

L'ordine del presente e il disordine del futuro - Saint Just (The Order of the Present is the Disorder of the Future), 1988, STONE,
MUSEUM PURCHASE, 1997.4

Crawling Lady Hare, 1997, GALVANIZED WIRE ON STEEL ARMATURE, MUSEUM PURCHASE, 1997.8

Sophie Ryder's *Crawling Lady Hare* is a larger than life half-woman half-hare shaped from tightly bundled galvanized wire and supported by a steel armature. With its blue-hued, densely wound wire surface, the sculpture takes to the woodland setting like a mythical figure in a mystical world. It is an Alice-in-Wonderland-like creature, full of fantasy and surreal mystique.

Born in London, England, and currently living and working in Gloucestershire, Sophie Ryder achieved national recognition at an early age. While still in her twenties she placed sculptures in some of Britain's finest outdoor collections and was honored with a one-person exhibition at the prestigious Yorkshire Sculpture Park, a show that received resounding critical acclaim. Her fantastical wire sculptures—minotaurs, dancing hares, and other creatures from her mythical imaginary world—are now sought by collectors around the world.

The sculptural technique that she has developed as her own, a painstaking process of building up figures with bundles of tangled wire, resembles drawing, each wire strand like the mark of a pencil. She cites as important influences some of the most profoundly creative artists of history: Goya, Picasso, and Henry Moore. Nevertheless, the forms she has developed and her methods of making them are distinctly her own.

Sophie Ryder created this piece at Cheekwood during a five-week residency in the Summer of 1997. She came with her husband, Harry Scott (a well respected photographer in his own right), and daughters Maude and Nell. In the course of that month she structured the piece around a welded steel armature, painstakingly building up the form—wire ball by wire ball—by weaving the galvanized wire bundles as though they were thread. Employees, trustees, and guests helped her crumple the steel wire, making the finished sculpture as much a monument to process as to product, at least for the fortunate who helped.

On creating the work on-site, Ryder comments, "To me, constructing pieces outside, in the setting they will remain in, is thrilling. Mostly sculpture is made in artists' studios and then delivered to their destinations. . . . The sculpture *[Crawling Lady Hare]* sits well in its surroundings, and knowing that the trees will grow and change in the different seasons adds to the excitement for me." In a more general comment on the process of creation, Ryder observes, "When a sculpture is complete and you stand back and look at it, if you get that tingly feeling that you get when you hear a beautiful piece of music, then that is when you know you are getting somewhere."

PHOTOGRAPH OF SOPHIE RYDER
COURTESY OF THE ARTIST. PHOTOGRAPH BY HARRY SCOTT.

JAMES TURRELL (AMERICAN, B. 1943)

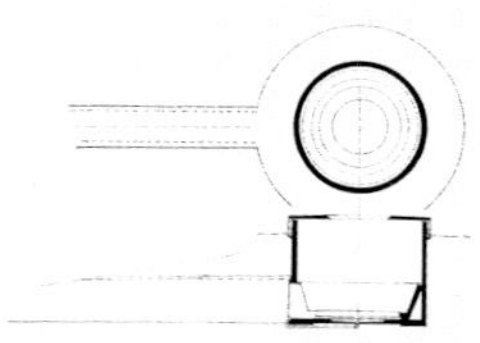

JAMES TURRELL,
SCHEMATIC DRAWINGS FOR *Blue Pesher,*
Museum Purchase 1999.4a

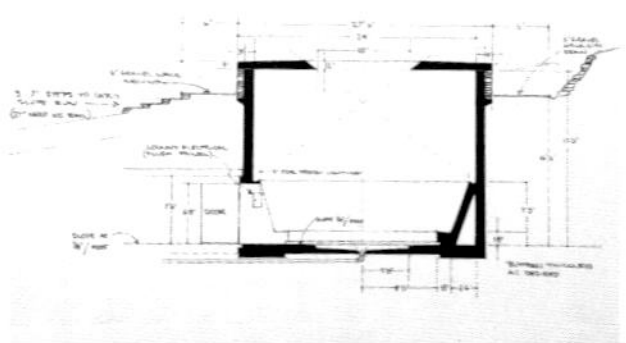

JAMES TURRELL,
SCHEMATIC DRAWINGS FOR *Blue Pesher,*
Museum Purchase 1999.4b

PHOTOGRAPH OF JAMES TURRELL
BY CELIA WALKER.

James Turrell's *Blue Pesher* is perhaps the most extraordinary sculpture on the Carell Woodland Sculpture Trail. As the trail ascends a steep hill, viewers come upon a door, much like a mine-shaft, leading to a forty-five-foot tunnel, brightly lit at the end. The tunnel opens into a cylindrical room, twenty feet in diameter, surrounded by high-backed benches. Everything is white. Seated on the bench, the viewer gazes upward toward what appears to be a painting of the sky but is really an open oculus, some ten feet wide. Neon lights hidden behind the ring of benches create the illusion, infusing the space with a sublime solemnity evocative of worship. The light is spectacular at sunset.

Turrell received a degree in psychology from Pomona College in Southern California in 1965. He also studied at the University of California, Irvine, and received his masters in art from the Claremont Graduate School in 1973. There he became fascinated with the power of light. Since then, his optical installations have appeared in major institutions around the world. Focused purely on light and space, Turrell's unique approach to sculpture defies tradition: "I have no object, no image, no point of focus . . . my interest is in plumbing the space."

According to *Time* magazine's critic Robert Hughes, "The medium of Turrell's work is perception itself; his art happens behind your eyes, not in front of them." Turrell has created a number of such "sky pieces"–in New York, Israel, Ireland, Italy, Los Angeles, and now Nashville–that place viewers in quasi-religious, meditative states. They are extremely serene environments that engage the viewer in the real and the spiritual. As Turrell observes, "It's not taking from nature as much as placing you in contact with it."

Turrell's great life work has been the Roden Crater, a vast volcanic cone in Arizona, the rim of which bulldozers have formed into a perfectly flat circle–a shape that frames the sky as a magnificent celestial sphere. In this crater will be observation rooms, tunnels, and reflecting pools, all focused on the sky. Hughes writes that they will "enable the visitor to experience the light of the sun, the moon, and the stars in isolated, concentrated ways: an instrument that will 'engage celestial events in light, so as to play the music of the spheres in light.'" It may be the most important sculpture of the late twentieth century.

Turrell is a remarkably learned and perceptive artist. His inspirations come from ancient cultures–the native peoples of Central America as well as Near Eastern civilizations–and from a profound knowledge of science and human perception. Turrell is a MacArthur Prize laureate (the so-called "Genius" award) as well as a Guggenheim Fellow and grant winner from the prestigious Dia Foundation. He is also an avid airplane pilot.

There is a magical quality to Turrell's light and space sculptures. As he says, "The best magic of all is the magic that is real."

Blue Pesher, 1997–1999, CONCRETE, NEON, AND MIXED MEDIA, MUSEUM PURCHASE, 1999.4

Tree Poem, 1998, ALUMINUM AND WOOD, MUSEUM PURCHASE, 1998.4

JOHN SCOTT (AMERICAN, B. 1940)

In *Tree Poem*'s skillful surface-finishing of shiny aluminum, John Scott emulates the moving shimmer of light in a breezy forest. Scott derived his abstracted trees from Cheekwood's own natural surroundings, using real trees as the inspiration for his forms. He replicated the tangled branches in an intricate abstract pattern. The viewer completes the piece through movement: *Tree Poem* is paper thin upon approach, then wide and complex as one views the metal trees straight on, the flickering sunlight making the branches appear to move.

A professor of fine arts at Xavier University in New Orleans, Louisiana, Scott believes in giving back to the city where he was born and raised and to the school where he received his education. In 1992 Scott was awarded the immensely prestigious MacArthur Prize, which, since 1981, has been awarded to writers, philosophers, scientists, artists, and other luminaries of extraordinary distinction. It is commonly known as the "Genius" prize. Scott is grateful for the prize but remains undeflected from his sense of self: "I'm glad somebody thinks I'm a genius, but it hasn't changed my perception of myself. . . . Nobody made me credible except myself."

The MacArthur Foundation was not the first to recognize Scott's genius, however. He has won numerous grants, awards, and fellowships and has appeared in a variety of major art publications. His sculptures are in major museums across America and in some of the finest private collections in the world, including those of Bill Cosby and Allen Toussaint. In 1996, his work was placed on exhibit in the White House.

The large proportions of Scott's kinetic sculptures seem ideally suited for the public domain. In his native New Orleans, public sculptures–such as *Ocean Song* in Woldenburg Park and *Poydras Street Dancing: Uptown Second Line*, which hangs from the ceiling at 1515 Poydras street–have contributed a great deal to Scott's public visibility. He has also created major public commissions for such prestigious clients as the Philadelphia Convention Center, the Boston Public Transport System, the New Orleans Museum of Art, and Hartsfield Airport in Atlanta.

Scott's aesthetic, while accessible, is extraordinarily complex. His pieces weave the urban experience with African heritage and the improvisational rhythms of New Orleans Jazz music. They are often emotional and thoughtfully humane. Scott considers himself a teacher as much as a sculptor, with a debt to younger, aspiring artists. He says, "I've been taught that if something is given to you, it's very important for you to pass it on. If I do something for a kid and he says 'Thank you,' I don't say 'You're welcome,' I say 'Pass it on.'"

PHOTOGRAPH OF JOHN SCOTT
BY JOHN WETENHALL.

Cheekwood Prime Matter—composed of copper, water, a cloud, and occasional bursts of fire—challenges traditional definitions of sculpture. It also serves as the monumental entrance to the sculpture trail.

Eric Orr arrived in Los Angeles in 1966 with a B.A. from the University of Cincinnati and a background in poetry and economics from New York's New School for Social Research. Orr had also spent a brief period studying at the University of Mexico and at the École de Paraphysiques in Paris. His education sparked an interest in metaphysics, which became the basis for his art.

Orr considered himself a protomaterialist, one concerned with the state prior to matter. His fascination with alchemy and the philosophical implications of purity and transformation led Orr to explore light, sound, and spectacle in a unique and compelling fashion.

Dry Ice and *Sky Lights*, sponsored by the Los Angeles Arts Commission, were Orr's first experiments with "protomaterialism." The first was an enormous maze of dry ice that gradually dematerialized, leaving only its vapors behind. The second was a long slit in the ground, nine feet deep, which emitted a glowing xenon light.

In 1991 Orr reached a new maturity and committed himself to the technical refinement of his art. *LA Prime Matter*, located on the plaza of the Mitsui Fudosan building, is a thirty-five foot construction of water that sends a column of fire shooting through the air every thirty minutes. This "light and space" sculpture won the LA City Beautiful Award. *Landmark Lumiere* was commissioned for the new Landmark Square Office Building in Long Beach. Orr lit the entire base of the building with white lights, then illuminated its glass sides with blue lights. The finishing touches are xenon lasers on the roof, creating a pyramid of light that shone like a beacon to planes flying overhead.

Orr's commissions can be found all around the world, from Japan and Korea to New Zealand and Europe, as well as throughout the United States. One of his most recent commissions adorns the entrance plaza to the new science center in Birmingham, Alabama.

In November of 1998, Eric Orr died of a heart attack in his studio in Los Angeles. He had only just completed *Cheekwood Prime Matter*.

PHOTOGRAPH OF ERIC ORR
COURTESY OF THE ARTIST.

Cheekwood Prime Matter, 1997–1998 (installed 1999), copper with water and fire, Museum Purchase, 1999.2

DETAIL: WILLIAM EDMONSON (AMERICAN 18-) *Bess and Joe*, c. 1935. limestone, Museum Purchase through the bequest of Anita Bevill McMichael Stallworth; and Gift of Salvatore J. Formosa, Sr.; Mrs. Pete A. Formosa, Sr.; Angelo Formosa, Jr.; and Mrs. Rose M. Formosa Bromley in loving memory of Angelo Formosa, Sr., wife Mrs. Katherine St. Charles Formosa, and Pete A. Formosa, Sr., 1993.2.3

All great art is the work
of the whole living creature, body and soul,
and chiefly the soul.

Herman Melville 1851-53

JACOB EICHHOLTZ, AMERICAN (1776-1842)

Jacob Eichholtz painted the portraits of established citizens in Pennsylvania, Delaware, and Maryland in the first half of the nineteenth century. Essentially self-trained, Eichholtz met Thomas Sully in 1808 while Sully was visiting Eichholtz's hometown of Lancaster, Pennsylvania. Sully gave Eichholtz, a tinsmith at the time, some old paintbrushes and started him on his way to a career in painting. Later Eichholtz met Gilbert Stuart, one of the leading East Coast portraitists, who gave Eichholtz advice and encouragement. Eichholtz's depiction of Jacob Barge Weidman (1789-1857), a lawyer from Lebanon, Pennsylvania, is one of over 250 portraits Eichholtz painted in his lifetime. The high color in his subject's face and the romantic character of the sitter suggest Sully's influence. Eichholtz's romantic realism appealed to successful members of the middle class who could not afford more celebrated portraitists such as Stuart or Sully.

Portrait of Jacob Barge Weidman,
C. 1812, OIL ON CANVAS, GIFT OF
MR. AND MRS. WALTER KNESTRICK, 1985.29.4

Portrait of Andrew Jackson, C. 1825,
OIL ON CANVAS, GIFT OF
MR. NEWELL J. WARD, JR., 1974.7.12

ARTIST UNKNOWN, AMERICAN (AFTER A. H. CORWINE)

Susan Symond, in her thesis, "Portraits of Andrew Jackson 1815-1845," discusses 128 known portraits of Andrew Jackson, 96 of which are bust portraits, such as this one. Ralph Earl painted 33 known portraits of Andrew Jackson, most of which were portrait busts. Symonds remarks that this type of informal portrait (what she calls a "simple" portrait as opposed to a full length or "high" portrait) was a logical choice for depicting a president associated with the common man. The Cheekwood portrait appears to have been painted after a portrait by Aaron H. Corwine (1802-1830), a Cincinnati artist who studied with Thomas Sully.

SAMUEL F. B. MORSE (AMERICAN, 1791-1872)

Samuel F. B. Morse's reputation as the inventor of the telegraph and Morse code have historically surpassed his reputation as an artist and arts leader during the nineteenth century. Throughout his career as artist and lecturer, he advocated the fine arts as tools to inspire moral and ethical values in Americans. Politically active, he helped found the National Academy of Design in 1825 and became New York University's first professor of art. As an accomplished portrait painter, he blended Gilbert Stuart's paint-layering techniques with strong lines that retain tactility and refinement. He created his own color schemes to invoke the specific mood he sought to portray. Morse had two brothers, Sidney Edwards, who founded, published, and edited the *New York Observer* and Richard Cary, who became a minister. Which brother is portrayed here remains unknown.

A picture then is not merely a copy of any work of Nature, it is constructed on the principles of nature. While its parts are copies of natural objects, the whole work is an artificial arrangement of them similar to the construction of a poem or a piece of music. -SAMUEL F. B. MORSE

Portrait of the Artist's Brother, N.D., OIL
ON CANVAS, GIFT OF MR. AND MRS. WALTER
KNESTRICK, 1985.29.7

JOHN WOOD DODGE (AMERICAN, 1807-1893)

John Wood Dodge was born in New York City and, at the outset of his career, apprenticed to a "tinner" (sign painter). Dodge became well-known for his dioramas and miniature portraits, such as this one. Portraiture accounts for close to half of all nineteenth-century American paintings, and posthumous or memorial portraits were common in the antebellum South, where child mortality ran high. When young Felix Grundy Eakin died at the age of three, his parents commissioned Dodge, who meticulously painted the child's likeness and the details of his accompanying objects: an urn, wilted flowers, and broken toys, all symbols of death.

Posthumous Likeness of Felix Grundy Eakin, 1846, OIL ON IVORY, TRANSFER FROM THE NASHVILLE MUSEUM OF ART, GIFT OF MRS. NANNIE EAKIN STEGER IN MEMORY OF HER DAUGHTER FELICIA STEGER GIBSON, 1960.2.72

DR. G.T. PENDLETON (AMERICAN, 19TH CENTURY)

The first American paintings appeared during the seventeenth century. Produced by untrained artists known as limner painters, portraits of this type demonstrated the sitters' wealth and prosperity. By commissioning such portraits, the rising American merchant class equated themselves with the middle class of England. Typical of limner work, this portrait of Elizabeth Yaeger by Dr. G. T. Pendleton-a physician in Oldham County, Kentucky, and Mrs. Yaeger's family's physician-is painted in flat forms and lacks tactility, weight, and classical modeling. This portrait is one of three of the Yaeger family that includes Elizabeth's father, Presley Nevel, and her stepmother, Susan Frances Hardin.

Portrait of Elizabeth O'Nora Yaeger, 1848, OIL ON LINEN, GIFT OF ANNE HOWE HARWELL, 1984.23.1

THOMAS HICKS (AMERICAN, 1823-90)

During the third quarter of the nineteenth century, Thomas Hicks was well regarded as a portraitist and landscape painter. Today, little is remembered about Hicks beyond his association with his Quaker cousin, the primitive artist Edward Hicks. After early study with his cousin, Thomas Hicks trained at the prestigious Pennsylvania Academy of the Fine Arts and studied abroad in the mid-1840s. Upon returning to New York, he became a member of the National Academy of Design, painting the likenesses of such luminaries as Abraham Lincoln, Harriet Beecher Stowe, and Henry Wadsworth Longfellow.

We do not know the name of the woman in Cheekwood's portrait, although we do know that she wears mourning attire. The penchant for mourning dress developed in England during the nineteenth century, reaching its peak in the Victorian era when the queen wore mourning clothes for her late husband, Prince Albert, for forty years until she died in 1901. "Widows weeds" allowed the wearers to remember their lost loved ones and to project a status allowing for such specialized clothing. The jet* ring, earrings, and necklace and the white lace worn in this portrait were appropriate attire for a woman in the second or third stage of mourning.** The red shawl recalls the blood of Christ; the cross is, in this case, especially appropriate in the light of the Christian doctrine of the resurrection, a time of reuniting with loved ones after death.

Portrait of a Lady with Lace Collar, 1854, OIL ON CANVAS, GIFT OF MR. AND MRS. HARRY SADLER, 1985.28.8

*JET IS A FORM OF SLATE MADE FROM FOSSILIZED DRIFTWOOD.

**THE FIRST STAGE OF MOURNING LASTED A MINIMUM OF ONE YEAR AND SEVERELY RESTRICTED COLOR AND FABRIC CHOICE. LATER MOURNING STAGES ALLOWED FOR ADDITIONAL FABRICS SUCH AS SILK AND GRADUALLY LESSENED COLOR RESTRICTIONS.

NATHANIEL CURRIER (AMERICAN, 1813-1888)

Clipper ships, built for speedy commercial use and getting their name from their reputation to "clip along," first appeared in Baltimore in 1812. The ships were designed with sharp front ends and tapering forms for greater speed through choppy seas. Passenger-ship speed was of the essence in the first half of the nineteenth century, when many Americans were going west to try their luck in the California Gold Rush. Railroad construction had only begun on the East Coast and Americans relied on ships to take them west by way of Cape Horn.

The Red Jacket was a well-known ship designed by Samuel A. Pook of Boston, the first independent marine architect in this country. It was named for a Seneca chief and British supporter who wore a bright red jacket in battle during the Revolutionary War. On its first voyage it made the transatlantic trip to Liverpool in thirteen days, one hour, twenty-five minutes, under the command of Capt. Asa Eldridge. Cheekwood's lithograph is the work of Nathaniel Currier, printed two years prior to his partnership with his brother-in-law, James Merritt Ives. It shows the Red Jacket on its subsequent voyage from Liverpool to Melbourne, Australia, and back, under the command of Capt. Samuel Reid. Typically, the route required ships to sail around the world in order to catch the favorable winds known as "westerlies." Ships traveled east, past the Cape of Good Hope, to Australia and again east across the Pacific Ocean and around Cape Horn. The Red Jacket made the trip to Australia in a record sixty-nine days, picked up 45,000 ounces of gold and returned in record time, beating its competitor, the Guiding Star, by nine days. J. B. Smith & Son, painters of the scene, show the clipper ship at Cape Horn, where the ship lost time among the icebergs.

Clipper Ship Red Jacket, 1855, COLORED LITHOGRAPH, GIFT OF MR. HANS ANDERSEN, 1998.11.6

Adelia Boisseau Warfield and Daughter, Huldah Belle, C. 1858, OIL ON CANVAS, GIFT OF MR. AND MRS. LESLIE CHEEK, JR., 1988.32.1-2

William Wallace Warfield and Son, [William Laban], C. 1858, OIL ON CANVAS, GIFT OF MR. AND MRS. LESLIE CHEEK, JR., 1988.32.1-2

ROBERT LOFTIN NEWMAN (AMERICAN, 1827-1912)

These dual portraits depict the Warfields, a handsome and successful farming family of Clarksville, Tennessee. The portraits are remnants of Robert Loftin Newman's surprisingly unsuccessful career in portrait painting. Newman structured these portraits with a sense of strong family ties and with symbols of the wealth and status the Warfields enjoyed. Adelia and Huldah Belle stand before a view of the Red River, representing the expanse of land their family owned. William and his son are posed in a study amidst worldly paraphernalia, such as a newspaper, a richly ornate vase, and fine furniture, demonstrating sophistication and knowledge. After several failed attempts at gaining consistent commissions, Newman finally abandoned portrait painting in 1873 to pursue his own vision-mysterious, figurative paintings inspired by the Romantics and other European movements-for which he would later become known.

ARTIST UNKNOWN, AMERICAN

At first glance, this painting appears out of perspective. A giant field worker, emerging from a thicket of stalks, towers over two gentlemen on horseback. Flagrantly enlarged fruit grows in the lush, green fields in front of an elegant Italianate mansion perched on a hilltop. This painting is an allegory, presented like a Garden of Eden, symbolizing the wealth and prosperity of Belmont's first owners, Joseph and Adelicia Acklen. The Acklens built Belmont with the romance of the Italian landscape in mind. They acquired the house plans during a trip to Italy and designed Belmont's surrounding gardens with a Mediterranean flair. They even derived the estate's name from Shakespeare's *The Merchant of Venice*. Adelicia, renowned for her beauty, charm, and impeccable style, was always at the center of the Nashville social scene, wearing the finest imported fashions and hosting legendary parties. After her husband's death in 1863, she successfully managed Belmont and plantations in Louisiana and Texas and became one of the wealthiest women in America. Today, the mansion stands at the center of Belmont University.

In Belmont is a lady richly left; And she is fair, and, fairer than that word, Of wondrous virtues. . . . -Shakespeare, The Merchant of Venice

Belmont, c. 1859-60, oil on canvas,
Gift of Naomi M. Kanaf in memory of her
husband Max Tendle, 1978.3.13

SANFORD R. GIFFORD (AMERICAN, 1823-1880)

*A Sketch of Cliffs in
Kaaterskill Clove,* 1863, oil on
canvas, Gift of
Mr. and Mrs. Walter
Knestrick, 1986.16.10

Sanford Gifford was a second-generation landscape painter whose favorite subject was his home area in the Hudson River Valley. After the Civil War, Americans became interested in exploring the more picturesque regions of the country, spurred on by popular magazine prints, improved railroad transportation, and a new enthusiasm for hiking. The Catskill Mountains, west of the Hudson River, were especially popular tourist sites. Advocates of the Romantic movement in art, literature, and philosophy associated the area's vistas with divine tranquillity. Gifford had grown up in the city of Hudson and knew the Catskill Mountains well. His favorite areas were the Kaaterskill Falls, the tallest waterfall in the state, and the Kaaterskill Clove, the dramatic valley at the foot of the falls. Seventeenth-century Dutch settlers believed the area to be the home of the devil, the clove thus named after the imprint made by the devil's cloven hoofs. Gifford painted the clove throughout his career from every imaginable angle. Here, Gifford shows us a close-up of the rocks, rather than the more typical view of the terrible ravine. Usually Gifford began with a pencil sketch, after which he would do an oil sketch, such as the one seen here. He would then create medium- and large-scale paintings from the sketches. The smaller oil sketch was affordable by middle-class patrons, often ending up in a private home or staying in the artist's estate, as this painting did. It displays the characteristics that made Gifford so successful: a calming, picturesque subject painted with invisible brush strokes and finished with a heavily varnished surface to approximate atmosphere.

ROBERT LOFTIN NEWMAN (AMERICAN, 1827-1912)

After his mother's death in 1873, Robert Loftin Newman moved permanently from Clarksville, Tennessee, to New York. There, he abandoned portrait painting to pursue his own artistic vision. Earlier, from 1854-1858, Newman had traveled and studied in France with William Morris Hunt, an influential American painter with strong ties to the Barbizon School, and had pursued an education uncommon among artists of that period. The Barbizon School condemned academic studio painting for its formulaic devices and false lighting. Instead, these artists painted outdoors, deriving their subject matter directly from nature-their forms often simplified and void of detail. These principles appealed to Newman, who combined them with the dramatic effects and obscure subject matter found in French Romanticism. Newman eventually developed a style distinct from any other artistic trends of the time and well-represented in *The Witching Hour*. In addition to looming landscapes, he ventured into mysterious and haunting figurative studies of mythological subjects, Biblical themes, and other literary sources, for which he is recognized today.

The Witching Hour, N.D., OIL ON CANVAS, GIFT OF MRS. WALTER SHARP, 1974.7.22

At college, I eagerly devoured histories, biographies, essays, poems recounting the glories and splendor of Titian, Rembrandt, Veronese, Leonardo da Vinci, Raphael, Corregio, Reubens, Holbein, Van Dyke and Guido and their host of followers.
-ROBERT LOFTIN NEWMAN

EASTMAN JOHNSON (AMERICAN, 1824-1906)

The Blacksmith Shop, N.D. OIL ON MASONITE, GIFT OF MR. AND MRS. WALTER KNESTRICK, 1981.26.9

Eastman Johnson's study for *The Blacksmith Shop* portrays a realistic scene of daily American life and is a product of Johnson's mid-career focus on genre painting from the 1850s to the 1880s-a period after his initial stint as a crayon limner, sketching portraits of his New England neighbors, and before his renowned era as a portrait painter of wealthy businessmen and American presidents.

Although Johnson generally adhered to the accepted style of his day, his choice of subject matter was personal and philosophical. Recalling Ralph Waldo Emerson, who said, "We have listened too long to the courtly muses of Europe," Johnson elaborated on his choice of subject matter, proclaiming:
We have yet had no genius in America with a tyrannous eye, which knew the value of our incomparable materials. . . . Our logrolling, our stumps, and their politics, our fisheries, our Negroes and Indians, our boats . . . the northern trade, the southern planting, the western clearing, Oregon and Texas, are yet unsung. Yet America is a poem in our eyes; its ample geography dazzles the imagination.

Much of Johnson's work was a study of that American poetry: farmers husking corn, people playing cards and making maple sugar, children playing in a hayloft, and cranberry pickers. Unlike many painters of his day, Johnson believed that all American subjects are worthy of portrayal in art, inspiring one critic to describe Johnson as "a chronicler of a phase of national life which is fast passing away."

WASHINGTON BOGART COOPER (AMERICAN, 1802-1889)

Washington Bogart Cooper, considered Tennessee's most prolific portrait painter, was primarily a self-taught artist. He began painting portraits at an early age on anything he could find-scraps of wood, barn doors, and the like. Cooper received no formal training until he was twenty-six, when an itinerant painter recognized his talent and took him in as an apprentice. That painter is thought to have been Ralph E. W. Earl, friend and official portraitist of Andrew Jackson. In 1831, Cooper departed for Philadelphia to study at the Pennsylvania Academy of the Fine Arts. While no records of his activities have been found, Cooper's subsequent paintings reveal the influence of renowned portrait painters Henry Inman and Thomas Sully. In *The Keith Children*, Cooper demonstrates his mastery of Thomas Sully's romantic and bright, cotton candy-like color palette, reminiscent of the eighteenth-century French rococo style while incorporating Inman's realist approach. After completing his education, Cooper returned to Nashville to open his own studio. He enjoyed an exceptionally successful career, producing portraits of governors and other prominent Tennessee residents.

The Keith Children, C. 1878, OIL ON CANVAS, TRANSFER FROM THE NASHVILLE MUSEUM OF ART. GIFT OF MR. AND MRS. MARTIN B. KEY IN MEMORY OF MRS. PERCY D. MADDIN, 1960.20

EDGAR JULIAN BISSELL (AMERICAN, 1856-1928)

The Humorist-Whiskey and Soda depicts a middle-aged man seated at an outdoor cafe enjoying a drink and the comics section of a French newspaper. Edgar Julian Bissell studied in Paris with Boulanger and Lefebvre, both popular teachers at that time, and adopted their academic style of painting. This piece was probably painted in Saint Louis, where Bissell moved after his return to the United States to teach at the Saint Louis School of Fine Art. Although the words painted on the windows behind him are in English ("books," "billiards," and "diner"), Bissell may have been reflecting on his stay in France. The setting appears to be a Parisian outdoor cafe scene, complete with a French newspaper, *Journal Amusant*.

The Humorist - Whiskey and Soda, 1885,
OIL ON PANEL, TRANSFER FROM THE NASHVILLE MUSEUM
OF ART, GIFT OF DR. AND MRS. GEORGE W. HALE, 1960.2.46

WILLIE BETTY NEWMAN (AMERICAN, 1863-1935)

Willie Betty Newman left her home in rural Tennessee in the early 1880s to study drawing and painting at the Art Academy of Cincinnati. There she earned a traveling scholarship that allowed her to study at the Académie Julian with Adolphe Bouguereau and other influential turn-of-the-century French artists. This scene was probably painted during that period of study, on a visit to Brittany. The idealized beauty of the peasant girl and the precise, invisible brush strokes used to create the scene reflect the influence of Bouguereau. Images such as *The Frugal Repast*, though overly sentimental to contemporary viewers, were popular subjects to the American public at the time this was painted.

The Frugal Repast, N.D., OIL ON CANVAS,
GIFT OF MR. AND MRS. IRBY SIMPKINS, 1990.3

ERNEST BLUMENSCHEIN (AMERICAN, 1874-1960)

Rising Wolf, 1898, GOUACHE
AND INDIA INK, GIFT OF MR. AND
MRS. JOHN A. HILL, 1991.10.16

Native American ceremonial dances have long been a popular subject among Western artists. These colorful events that marked the seasons and the important moments of Indian religion were depicted by Henry Balink, Ernest Blumenschein, Eanger Irving Couse, Fritz Scholder, John Sloan, and many others. Cheekwood's collection contains three depictions of ceremonial dances, by Harrison Begay, Ernest Blumenschein, and Fritz Scholder. During the winter of 1897-1898, Blumenschein was working in New Mexico and Arizona on assignment as an illustrator for *McClure's* magazine. This drawing of *Rising Wolf* may have been made on that trip or during the summer of 1898, when Blumenschein returned to the West with his studio mate, Bert Phillips. Prior to venturing West, Blumenschein had studied at New York's Art Students League, where teachers such as William Merritt Chase stressed the importance of working from life. It's likely that Blumenschein wanted to make clear the derivation of this drawing because he added the inscription "from photo" at the bottom, along with the date. Indeed, the detail and finish of the drawing, which could have come only from a photograph, suggest that the image was created for illustration and was probably part of his *McClure's* assignment.

JOHN CHRISTEN JOHANSEN (AMERICAN, 1876-1964)

John Christen Johansen was an American painter and teacher born in Copenhagen, Denmark, in 1876. He studied with such luminaries as James McNeil Whistler and Frank Duveneck at the Art Institute of Chicago and the Académie Julian in Paris. By 1904 he lived in New York and taught at the Art Students League. In 1911 the National Academy made him an associate and in 1915 an academician. Although Johansen is known primarily as an impressionistic portraitist, his work is subdued in color and brushwork. *The Story Book* depicts a mother (or perhaps a grandmother or aunt) and daughter reading a book together. The gaze of the little girl, who looks up from the book and out directly at the viewer (or artist), suggests she has become momentarily distracted from the book and perhaps more interested in the artist and the activity of painting hers and her mother's portrait.

The Story Book, 1905, OIL ON CANVAS, MUSEUM PURCHASE, 1982.23.2

JOHN SINGER SARGENT (AMERICAN, 1856-1925)

Falconieri Gardens, Frascati, 1907, OIL ON CANVAS, GIFT OF MR. AND MRS. WALTER KNESTRICK, 1985.29.11

John Singer Sargent is the most well known society portraitist of the late nineteenth century. The lavish elegance of his paintings brought him unrivaled success in America and Europe, and his portraits of the wealthy and privileged convey with brilliant bravura the glamour and opulence of high society. However, he also loved painting landscapes, and around 1907 he began taking fewer and fewer commissions for society portraits. This landscape of the Villa Falconieri Gardens, near Rome, surveys a large garden and fountain. Note the large olive tree in the foreground, and look carefully for the water fountain, behind and to the left of the tree. The background is composed of cypress trees. The Villa Falconieri was built at the end of the sixteenth century by Cardinal Farnese and later renovated by the Falconieri family, who commissioned the famous Baroque architect Francesco Borromini to renovate it in the eighteenth century.

WILLIAM WASHINGTON GIRARD (AMERICAN, 1873-1931)

Moonlit Landscape, N.D., OIL ON BOARD, ANONYMOUS GIFT

Turn-of-the-century American artists witnessed a rapid change in the direction, goals, and values of the fine arts community. Some artists chose to emulate the radical and rebellious concepts of the European avant-garde, introduced in New York through the 1913 Armory Show. Others remained committed to traditional styles and subjects inspired by academic ideals. Resisting the influx of cubism, fauvism, and other movements overseas, William Washington Girard, a Tennessee artist, wanted to paint the natural world around him. He captured the same sensitivity to nature found in paintings of the Hudson River School by depicting the unindustrialized midwestern terrain in a spiritual manner. In this particular nightscape, a lake isolated between two mountain peaks reflects the moon's beams. The scene is, at once, hollow and solitary, but somehow peaceful and mysterious.

New York in the Snow, N.D., OIL ON BOARD, GIFT OF MR. AND MRS. WALTER KNESTRICK, 1985.29.1

AARON BOHROD (AMERICAN, 1907-1992)

Aaron Bohrod began his art career deeply interested in painting Wisconsin landscapes with the same fervor as the Regionalists, a group of artists patriotically moved to paint the American scene. An experiment with encaustics led him to a life-long pursuit of painting small, realistic still lifes. He was to become one of the country's premier trompe l'oeil still-life painters. Bohrod was born in Chicago and studied at the Art Institute of Chicago and with John Sloan at the Art Students League in New York. Bohrod considered Sloan his greatest inspiration and took to heart Sloan's commandment to "draw everything you can see or imagine or dream of, and draw in every conceivable way and with every conceivable tool." *New York in the Snow* was perhaps painted during his tenure at the Art Students League in New York with Sloan. The painting has the hallmark characteristics of Sloan's early Ashcan work: loose brush strokes and a dark palette.

LEON KROLL (AMERICAN, 1884-1974)

Leon Kroll, an artist-teacher and a native New Yorker, studied at the Art Students League with John Twachtman and at the National Academy of Design. He had his first one-man show in New York in 1911 and was included in the important Armory Show of 1913, which introduced modern art to America. Although Kroll is chiefly known for his naturalistic cityscapes and industrial scenes treated in a loose, painterly style, he painted many portraits and nudes in a tighter, stylized fashioned. During his long life, Kroll worked for the WPA and painted murals for the Justice Department in Washington, D.C., for the War Memorial Building in Worcester, Massachusetts, and for Johns Hopkins University. *Upper Broadway* is typical of Kroll's cityscapes, with its innovative use of painterly brushwork in an impressionistic fashion.

Upper Broadway, c. 1910, OIL ON WOOD, GIFT OF MR. AND MRS. JOHN A. HILL, 1975.1.2

Girl with Japanese Lanterns, c. 1912, OIL ON CANVAS, GIFT OF 1996 AND 1997 COLLECTORS' GROUPS WITH MATCHING FUNDS FROM THE BEQUEST OF ANITA BEVILL McMICHAEL STALLWORTH, 1997.3.1

EVERETT SHINN (AMERICAN, 1876-1953)

Everett Shinn was a master at catching a fleeting instant on paper or canvas. In an age before newspaper photography, Shinn's early training as a newspaper illustrator taught him to portray daily metropolitan dramas, such as fires and traffic accidents, rapidly and accurately. Shinn's focus changed after an extended visit to Paris with fellow-Eight member George Luks. The trip led Shinn into a lifelong affair with the theater, increasingly his favorite subject after 1903. Shinn's ability to capture a dramatic moment was well suited to theater scenes, now augmented by the unnatural coloration produced by stage limelight. Typical of his artistic technique is this 1912 *Girl with Japanese Lanterns,* with its stage-like setting and garish lighting. Japanese lanterns were used as decorations at festivities and theatrical performances after the East opened to international trade in the last quarter of the nineteenth century. Their presence suggests that a party or play is taking place, possibly at the small theater Shinn built behind his home at 112 Waverly Place in Greenwich Village.

CHARLES HAWTHORNE (AMERICAN, 1872-1930)

Charles Hawthorne spent the last thirty years of his life teaching art at the Cape Cod School of Art, the school he began in Provincetown, Massachusetts, in 1899. His self-portrait contains the elements of his style, which emphasized light and color over line. The Cape Cod School was the first plein air school in America, its artists painting out of doors as the Impressionists did in France. Having studied Impressionism in Europe with William Merritt Chase, Hawthorne combined the Impressionists' interest in atmosphere with his own passion for the common man, whom he represented in his paintings of the rugged fishermen of the Massachusetts coastline.

Self-Portrait, N.D., OIL ON BOARD, GIFT OF DR. A. EVERETTE JAMES, JR., 1986.20.1

GUY PÉNE DU BOIS (AMERICAN, 1884-1958)

On the Roof, N.D., OIL ON BOARD, GIFT OF MR. AND MRS. WALTER KNESTRICK, 1986.16.19

In this painting by Guy Péne du Bois, a young woman clothed in a negligée stands on the roof of her apartment. The city shimmers softly and noiselessly behind her, while the moonlight highlights her form. Péne du Bois, although primarily an art and literature critic, studied painting at the New York School of Art under the guidance of William Merritt Chase, Robert Henri, and Kenneth Hayes Miller. He combined the fluid, impressionistic techniques advocated by Chase with Henri's social realism to depict often satirical and sometimes melancholic scenes of upper-class society, focusing primarily on women. As in many of his paintings, the lady in *On the Roof* appears statuesque, frozen, almost unreal. Enveloped in solitude on her rooftop haven, she remains mysterious.

OSCAR BLUEMNER (AMERICAN, B. GERMANY, 1867-1938)

Bloomfield, 1917, PENCIL ON PAPER, GIFT OF MRS. CATHERINE FERRIS BEASLEY, 1975.5.2

The simple forms in Oscar Bluemner's pencil sketch of Bloomfield, New Jersey, divide this composition into abstract shapes that hover and overlap in a manner akin to the spiritually inspired geometric compositions of Wassily Kandinsky and Arthur Dove. The white horizontal line of the road, the full moon, and the foreground's vertical white space exist not as realistic renderings meant to convey a record of place but as geometric points of entry amid a flurry of penciled strokes. This attention to abstract forms relates directly to Bluemner's admiration for American modernists like Georgia O'Keeffe, as well as to his belief that "whatever inner impulse we address toward nature is abstract. Thus a landscape as a motive for expression undergoes a free transformation from objective reality to a subjective realization of personal vision." When viewing *Bloomfield,* one can imagine Bluemner's hand moving rapidly to capture the image in one sitting. These crosshatched pencil strokes take full advantage of drawing's immediacy and intimacy, furthering the viewer's understanding of Bluemner's personal vision.

OSCAR E. BERNINGHAUS (AMERICAN, 1874-1952)

Scout of the Caravan, N.D., OIL ON LINEN, GIFT OF THE ESTATE OF JOHN A. AND MARGARET HILL, 1994.19.22

Oscar Berninghaus became fascinated with the frontier after receiving a free pass to travel west on the Denver and Rio Grande Railroad. Like many Western artists, Berninghaus had been working as an illustrator, and railroads often traded passage to artists for advertising images. Unlike most of the highly trained East Coast artists who came west at the turn of the century, Berninghaus was essentially self-taught, except for three terms of night classes at the St. Louis School of Fine Arts. Much of his early style, evident in *Scout of the Caravan,* was due to the influence of Charles Russell, who shared a studio with Berninghaus in St. Louis in 1912. Russell's flat, decorative style and nostalgic cowboy subject matter is echoed in this painting. The scout pauses to ascertain if the road ahead is safe for the wagon train, seen receding in the distant hills. The scout's heroic character is suggested by his determined face and by the defensive positioning of his rifle. Berninghaus abandoned this type of subject and loosened his brush stroke after 1925, when he moved to Taos and came under the influence of the modern cotérie residing there.

EANGER IRVING COUSE (AMERICAN, 1866-1936)

The Fire Maker, N.D., OIL ON CANVAS, GIFT OF THE ESTATE OF JOHN A. AND MARGARET HILL, 1994.19.27

Of all of the first generation of artists to settle in Taos, New Mexico, Irving Couse borrowed most heavily from traditional academic sources. His style was largely shaped at New York's National Academy of Design and at the Académie Julian in Paris, where he studied with Adolph Bouguereau. Bouguereau taught a painstaking technique that he used to produce elegant, idealized subjects. He taught his students to begin with a preparatory drawing, which they would then transfer to canvas by pencil and T square. Only then was the student to apply paint to canvas to fill in the drawn subjects. No brush strokes were to be visible to distract the eye. The finished painting would be a balanced, symmetrical composition of idealized figures.

Couse's *Fire Maker* contains all of these elements and is typical of the artist's work. Most of Couse's paintings are similarly small indoor images of a single, semi-clothed Native American engaged in some domestic task. Here, the figure tends to a central fire that allows Couse to highlight his idealized subject. Two ears of corn in the foreground suggest that this is not a plains hunter but a peaceful pueblo farmer. At far left a painted ceramic pot balances the squatting figure and signifies his artistic interests. Couse continued to paint these small, beautiful canvases throughout his life and to sell them in New York City.

WILLIAM POSEY SILVA (AMERICAN, 1859-1948)

Garden of Dreams, N.D., OIL ON CANVAS, TRANSFER FROM THE NASHVILLE MUSEUM OF ART, 1960.2.107

Stepping into his father's trade, William Posey Silva began his career painting chinaware. After graduating from the University of Virginia, he applied his talents at his father's studio until 1887, when he was able to open his own studio in Chattanooga, Tennessee. By 1900, his interests shifted to easel painting, and he spent the next six summers in Ipswich, Massachusetts, studying with Arthur Wesley Dow. At the time, many American art students spent part of their education attending one of the great art academies in Europe. Silva spent 1907-1909 at the famous Académie Julian. He took special interest in the painting techniques of the French Impressionists, adopting their airy, pastel palette. Also influenced by tonalism, he emphasized the effect of sunlight on objects. In Silva's *Garden of Dreams* the Impressionistic color palette is muted and grayed. Tonalist devices are used to portray the diffusion of sunlight in the hazy, vaporous summer heat of the South. Spanish moss drips from the massive trees. The subdued tones and filmy pictorial atmosphere characterize a walk through a dreamy, surreal garden.

EUGENE ATGET (FRENCH, 1857-1927)

Eugene Atget's images of shop windows are particularly important to his body of work because they emerged late in his career and asserted his new-found interest in giving visual importance to reflections. Atget photographed this shop during an era when department stores in Paris, with their variety of goods, had become a popular alternative to boutiques.

The compositional elements in the reflection are excessive and create a sense of commotion, reflective of the accelerated pace of Paris in the postwar age. Atget felt that many of that era's progressive attitudes-especially in the hands of civic bureaucrats-threatened the very existence of the architecture and social structure of old Paris. This threat to the historic district inspired Atget to record antique quarters of Paris voraciously until his death in 1927.

Atget's use of a simple documentary style during an era when many photographers strove to create soft-focus, painterly photographs caught the eye of young photographers of the 1920s and 1930s. Atget's influence on this next generation, including American luminaries Berenice Abbott and Walker Evans, has since justified numerous photographers and art historians in naming Atget the father of modern photography.

Printed by Berenice Abbott, (1898-1991). *MAGASINS DU BON MARCHÉ,* 1926-27, GELATIN SILVERPRINT, GIFT OF MS. JEAN RANKIN BURN, 1984.10.6.6

MAYNARD DIXON (AMERICAN, 1875-1946)

First Pacific Railroad, 1930, GOUACHE AND PENCIL ON PAPER, GIFT OF THE ESTATE OF JOHN A. AND MARGARET HILL, 1994.19.7

Maynard Dixon's *First Pacific Railroad* is a portrait of progress. The focus is on the train as it enters the frame's foreground and crosses the bridge, as a diminutive wagon and lone rider-serving as reminders of the past-begin to exit the landscape. Dixon rendered the old and the new in equally flattering light, while making clear that the force represented in the train is overwhelming. Dixon's even-handed treatment of the subject matter leaves it to the viewer to grapple with the pros and cons of progress.

Dixon, who at a young age was encouraged by Western artist Frederic Remington to record life in the Southwest, began to create illustrations for newspapers and magazines, including the *San Francisco Examiner,* which he joined in 1900. Dixon's desire to portray with honesty the country he loved, however, led him to abandon commercial work in 1921, feeling that he was "being paid to lie about the West, the country I know and care about."

A.C. WEBB, JR. (AMERICAN, 1888-1975)

A. C. Webb's portrait of the Chrysler Building recalls the majesty and glory of the skyscraper during the Depression. Commissioned by Walter P. Chrysler and designed by William Van Allen in 1930, the Chrysler Building was a natural choice for Webb. The building was inspired by Chrysler's desire for a structure higher than the Eiffel Tower to parlay into selling cars. It was the tallest structure in the world until that honor was usurped with the completion of the Empire State Building a mere one year later.

The sleek black assertiveness of the gargoyle reigns over New York, seen here as a Mecca of architectural proliferation, honoring modern architecture and the capitalistic endeavors that they house. Webb's choice of skyscraper as subject, however, did not originate from an avidly modernist viewpoint nor from an idealized love of the industrial age. More likely, he merely transposed his tendency to romanticize architecture that evokes, in such American skyscrapers as the Chrysler building, the monumental cathedrals of France.

Chrysler Building Gargoyle, N.D. GOUACHE OVER PHOTO DRAWING, GIFT OF ELLENNA WEBB DOUGLAS, 1984.14.51

Reciline Man, c. 1930s, LIMESTONE,
GIFT OF MICHAEL LEBECK IN MEMORY OF
SIDNEY MTTRON HIRSCH, 1973.4.8

WILLIAM EDMONDSON (AMERICAN, 1874-1951)

Recumbent, eyes closed, perhaps in meditation, and in a rather formal pose, this is the only known completely nude male, with its overt revelation of genitalia, that Edmondson ever carved. The bushy hair and faint markings of a Vandyke beard suggest a likeness to Sidney Mttron Hirsch, who inspired the piece. Hirsch was the spiritual guru of the Fugitives, a poetry circle anchored at Vanderbilt University including, among others, John Crowe Ransom, Robert Penn Warren, and Allen Tate. Although not at Vanderbilt himself, Hirsch convinced the group to publish their work in what became their famous poetry magazine, *The Fugitive*, from 1922-1925.

Hirsch lived six blocks from Edmondson's Fourteenth Avenue South home. Intrigued by the backyard filled with stone creatures, Hirsch, a gregarious man by nature, introduced himself to Edmondson. The congenial Edmondson welcomed him, and the two became acquaintances. Through Hirsch, Edmondson met fellow Fugitive Alfred Starr and, later, Louise Dahl-Wolfe. Dahl-Wolfe would become instrumental in placing Edmondson's work in the Museum of Modern Art in 1937, thus becoming the first African-American artist to have a one-man exhitition there. Of all the Fugitives, Hirsch was most interested in Far Eastern religions and the etymological and symbolic meanings of words. He often experimented with creating his own symbolic language, signs of which this sculpture may depict. A mysterious shield-like emblem on the stomach may simply be the striations of well-defined abdominal muscles or may point to an unknown symbolism. The figure's backside reveals overt markings unlike any other in Edmondson's work. An arrow's endpoint coincides with the base of the spine, and its shaft encloses nine barely discernible glyphs running down the spinal column. Unusual also for its lack of a pedestal, the piece is completely freestanding.

WILLIAM EDMONDSON (AMERICAN, 1874-1951)

In this depiction of Eve, each aspect of the first woman has been considered, every detail thoughtfully bestowed. The unique, crown-like hairstyle draws attention to Eve's head and complements her dramatically large, oval earrings. Edmondson's trademark texturing contrasts the hair with smooth facial skin and the patterning on her cape. Her eyes, nose, and mouth are all carefully detailed. Her left hand gently touches her breast perhaps indicating fecundity as World Mother. Playfully, a sleeve covers only her right arm, and a short cape stops just short of covering her bare derriere. Capes or robes were signs of royalty or significance for Edmondson, as evident in *Girl with Cape* and several of his angels. Eve's maple leaf does not so much cover as it draws attention. This is Eve full of sensuous qualities and sexuality. Edmondson presents woman standing firmly on her own, yet also on the proverbial pedestal, as icon, as Eve, as Mother of all.

Eve, c. 1930s, LIMESTONE,
GIFT OF MRS. ALFRED STARR, 1964.10

WILLIAM EDMONDSON (AMERICAN, 1874-1951)

Standing on her pedestal, *Girl with Cape* features dramatic, forthright body language-head up, arms folded in front as if she is waiting for something to occur, torso squared precisely forward. Held in place by a simple bow, the cape, rectangular and accented with rounded ninety-degree angles, envelops the body and provides something of a shield. Voluminous hair squarely adorns the head and ripples down her back into a neatly tied body-length braid of hair. These features and body language suggest that perhaps this young woman is prepared to accept any challenge and to face the world head on.

Girl with Cape, c. 1930s, limestone, Gift of the estate of Elizabeth Lyle Starr, 1982.8.1

HENRY C. BALINK (AMERICAN, 1882-1963)

Born in Amsterdam, Hendricus Cornelius Balink seemed an unlikely candidate to become a Western artist. But after a brief stay in New York he moved to New Mexico in 1917, drawn by the elemental scenery and native culture. Balink spent the rest of his life documenting Native American culture from his home base in Santa Fe. Like so many turn-of-the-century artists, Balink was trained in Europe and on the East Coast. He required several years to adapt his painting style to the very different climactic conditions and grand-scale scenery of the West.

This portrait of Little Bear, though undated, is stylistically related to Balink's work after 1930, when his palette brightened and his brush stroke became visible. Taking advantage of the chief's headdress, Balink draws the viewer's eye to his subject's weathered yet dignified face. Over the years Balink reportedly persuaded subjects from sixty-three different tribes to pose, creating an important visual series of a vanishing culture.

Portrait of Little Bear, N.D., oil on linen, Gift of Mr. and Mrs. John A. Hill, 1991.10.13

ELLA S. HERGESHEIMER (AMERICAN, 1873-1943)

Ella Hergesheimer-with one hand propped mightily on her hip, the other holding a paint brush, and her head cocked with a knowing smile-portrays herself as a person full of verve, style, and accomplishment. Hergesheimer's confidence was likely the result of her early exposure to art as the great-great-granddaughter of famed American painter Charles Willson Peale and of her extensive training, which included studies under the influential American artist William Merritt Chase and additional education in Germany, Spain, and France.

In *Self-Portrait* Hergesheimer is as stylish as she is confident. Her fashionable attire, which includes a colorful hat, a loosely-draped floral scarf, and a boldly wrought necklace, projects the independent flair of many women during the 1930s. Conversely, the painting's pastel hues and the flowing fabric of Hergesheimer's dress allude to the traditional feminine qualities of congeniality and tenderness. The dual nature of gracious woman and assertive artist is summed up in the painting's foreground with a black cat and a painter's palette. By choosing the feline, a symbol of feminine wiles, and the palette, a tool of the painter, Hergesheimer left little doubt that she valued, above all else, her possession of femininity and creative drive.

Self-Portrait, 1931, oil on canvas, Transfer from The Nashville Museum of Art, 1960.2.12

GERARD CURTIS DELANO (AMERICAN, 1890-1972)

The title, *Centaurs of the Canyon*, connects Navajo culture with Greek mythology. Centaurs were depicted in Greek literature and art as creatures combining the torso and head of a man with the body of a horse. The most famous of the centaurs was Chiron, who was tutored by the gods Apollo and Artemis in medicine, music, hunting, and war and who passed his knowledge along to Achilles and Aesculapius. Traditionally, the Navajos also excelled in these arts. Struck by the stark Arizona landscape and colorful clothing worn by the Navajos, Delano fused the monumental, arid surroundings with his reverence for the ancient tribe in bright, smooth, purified colors and noble, serene pictorial arrangements.

The Navajo people are a proud and beautiful race of great dignity. It is my idea to show them as I know them. There are few poorer anywhere, yet it would be difficult to find a happier lot, and I wonder if there is not a lesson in this for all of us. -GERARD CURTIS DELANO

Centaurs of the Canyon, N.D., OIL ON CANVAS PANEL, GIFT OF THE ESTATE OF JOHN A. AND MARGARET HILL, 1994.19.30

LOUISE DAHL-WOLFE (AMERICAN, 1895-1989)

Night Bathing, 1939, GELATIN SILVERPRINT, GIFT OF THE ARTIST, 1984.24.50

Night Bathing features dramatic lighting, appropriated imagery from art history, and a subtly conveyed romantic mood. What would seem forced in lesser hands becomes a delicate suggestion in Dahl-Wolfe's, as the beauty of a Greek goddess is compared to the elegance of the modern American woman. An early appropriator of art history, Dahl-Wolfe used other works of art as backdrops to echo a model's form or style of dress. *Night Bathing* exemplifies her approach by featuring a Greco-Roman sculpture in the foreground that echoes the pose of the casually posed fashion model. Note how Dahl-Wolfe tempered the lighting to emphasize the model but also to convey the romantic mood of a late night dip in the pool. Dahl-Wolfe once observed that "the camera is a medium of light, that one actually paints with light."

PERLE FINE (AMERICAN, 1905-1988)

Perle Fine moved to New York from Boston in 1928 to study painting. In the 1930s she met Hans Hofmann, one of the leaders of a group of abstract expressionists that included Jackson Pollock and Arshile Gorky. Also known as Action Painters or the New York School, these artists injected their nonobjective paintings with deep personal emotion to create powerful, expressive art during the 1940s and early 1950s. Fine studied with Hofmann at the Art Students League and later in the school Hofmann founded near Fine's own Tenth Street flat. Artists were drawn to this Greenwich Village area for its low rents and for the camaraderie shared among the residents. Fine was one of the few women accepted by the Tenth Street "club." Her *Pure Myth* shows the influence of Gorky's paintings of the 1940s in their dream imagery and rounded, biomorphic forms. Fine and others attempted to tap subconscious memories in their paintings, often producing mythic, universal images in the process.

Pure Myth, 1948-49, OIL ON CANVAS, GIFT OF THE BEREZOV FAMILY, 1994.21

Untitled, 1955-56, From the Pittsburgh essay, gelatin silver print, Gift of Mr. Fred Nederlander, 1985.9.1.6

W. EUGENE SMITH (AMERICAN, 1918-78)

Eugene Smith's photograph of two women in a Pittsburgh hat shop reveals how he could make himself invisible to others in spite of their knowledge of his presence. Both women are absorbed, one engrossed in assessing a hat and the other glancing toward a young woman whose reflection we see in the mirror. This image is from the Pittsburgh photographic essay begun around 1954 with the help of a Guggenheim grant. That project's size and scope made it Smith's most ambitious work.

As early as 1936, in a letter to his mother, Smith spoke of this goal to capture the unadorned reality of life: "My station in life is to capture the action of life . . . in other words life as it is. A true picture, unposed and real." Smith eventually took this credo to national magazines such as *Newsweek* and *Life*. Considered by editors and photographers to be a maverick of photojournalism, Smith's rebellious reputation stemmed primarily from his insistence on editorial control over the magazine layouts of his work. Most notable for his success in creating photographic essays, Smith advocated abandoning simple chronology in favor of layouts focused on visual dynamics through symbolic juxtapositions. Smith once compared the arrangement of photographic essays to that of a symphony's emotional highs and lows.

WERNER WILDNER (AMERICAN, B. 1925)

Ceremonial Beast, 1958, oil on panel , Gift of Dr. and Mrs. Benjamin H. Caldwell, Jr., 1976.12.33

The surreal imagery of Werner Wildner's *Ceremonial Beast* is a fantastical cacophony of images from mythology and ancient Western civilization. In this painting Wildner creates his own version of the Greek mythological creature the Centaur and surrounds it with ancient references, from the braids and horns of Viking legend to the ceremonial laurels of Roman culture. Wildner manages to balance these disparate symbols harmoniously, however, by pairing elements that enhance the image's dream-like qualities.

These paired elements mirror each other throughout *Ceremonial Beast*, introducing the eye to such particularly symbolic comparisons as the human head over against the diminutive twig, which draws our attention to the disproportionate dominance of the body over the head. Wildner's symbolism seems, consequently, to emphasize the eternal battle between the desires of the animal (horse half) and the voice of the intellect (human half), reminding us of the fragile line between the rituals of civilized life and the natural world.

Werner Wildner, a child of German immigrants, moved to Nashville from Detroit in 1940. After the war he returned to Detroit, where he received his only formal art training during a short stint at Mienzinger Art School. He then moved back to Nashville and worked as a commercial artist in the late 1940s, dedicating his time exclusively to his own work by the 1950s. Wildner received significant regional attention with a 1962 solo exhibition at the Cheekwood Museum of Art. His work can be found in the collections of the Smithsonian Institution, Washington D. C., and the High Museum of Art, Atlanta.

JACK BEAL (AMERICAN, B. 1931)

Still Life with Snow Shovel, 1965.
OIL ON CANVAS, GIFT OF THE AMERICAN
ACADEMY AND INSTITUTE OF ARTS AND
LETTERS, NEW YORK CITY, HASSAM AND
SPEICHER PURCHASE FUND, 1988.1

Still Life with Snow Shovel is one of the first of several canvases that Jack Beal created in what would become his mature, representational style. Beal used his early training in Abstract Expressionism to compose colors, patterns, and light in this realistic still life. In juxtaposing certain colors and hues, Beal adds an optical illusion of pulsing movement to the painting's realism. Although deemed a still life, the shovel, furniture, and flannel shirt metaphorically serve as features on the face of suburbia, making this painting an allegory of American life.

Beal's turn to realism began in 1962 with a sudden urge "to get more natural form and color" back into his paintings, although he "had no notion at all of becoming a representational painter." Like many young artists of the early 1960s, Beal became progressively enamored of representation's refreshing departure from an art world dominated by the torrid brush strokes of Willem de Kooning and the colorful compositions of Morris Louis and Kenneth Noland.

EMIL BISTTRAM, (AMERICAN, B. HUNGARY, 1895-1976)

Hungarian-born Emil Bisttram explored many means of expression ranging from abstraction to realism during his artistic career. After receiving a Guggenheim fellowship, he moved from New York to New Mexico in the 1930s to study fresco painting with Diego Rivera. Influenced by the Native American culture that surrounded him, he developed a philosophy that art should inspire higher spirituality. Using native scenery and images of local people, he aspired to create new modes of expression and to capture a universal quality in his work. A popular subject for many artists and an obsession for Georgia O'Keeffe, the church of San Francisco de Asis at Ranchos de Taos, New Mexico, is a striking southwestern architectural monument in its own right. Bisttram depicted the Ranchos church with gothic, mystical force.

Ranchos Church, 1974,
WATERCOLOR, GIFT OF THE ESTATE
OF JOHN A. AND MARGARET HILL,
1994.19.5

IDA KOHLMEYER (AMERICAN, 1912-1997)

Symbols 81-5, 1981, ACRYLIC, PENCIL,
AND CHARCOAL ON CANVAS, MUSEUM
PURCHASE WITH FUNDS PROVIDED
THROUGH THE EXCHANGE CLUB
CHARITIES, 1982.15.14

Ida Kohlmeyer née Rittenberg, was born and reared in New Orleans. She did not develop an interest in art until the age of thirty-five. Encouraged by many, her strongest support came from sculptor George Rickey who wrote to her, "You are too independent, too ambitious, and too strong a personality to be content with eclecticism."

Symbols 81-5 stands as a neo-Formalist sampler, an inventory of the abstract artist's alphabet. Where the Abstract Expressionists sought to convey philosophical and emotional conceits through the liquid movement of the violent brush stroke, subsequent artists contented themselves with formal exercises that merely listed the possibilities. After Roy Lichtenstein famously and humorously deconstructed the personal brush mark with *Brushstrokes,* 1965, artists were freed (or imprisoned) to explore their own idioms of mark making. The title, *Symbols 81-5,* simply affirms the notion that these are only symbols, just marks on a surface that contain nothing metaphysical in and of themselves. Kohlmeyer's medley of signifiers and vibrant surfaces celebrate the personal excursion into the romantic philosophy of painting, and painting alone.

MICHAEL COLEMAN (AMERICAN, B.1946)

Coleman places this compact group of sheep, with their dense rounded forms, in a pastoral setting, reminiscent of traditional landscape painting. The elliptical roundness of these woolly animals, however, has often attracted modern artists who, like Coleman, are drawn to the sheep's visually formal and universally symbolic qualities-Christianity, peace, blind obedience, and, when counted, a solution to insomnia.

In 1980 British sculptor Henry Moore (1898-1986) devoted an entire sketchbook to sheep. Initially a project to kill time while his exhibit was being installed, the sketchbook reflects the evolution of Moore's awareness from a purely formal interest in their shapes to a curiosity about their individual personalities: "At first I saw [the sheep] as shapeless balls of wool with a head and four legs. Then I began to realize that underneath all that wool was a body . . . and that each sheep had its individual character."

German conceptual artist Joseph Beuys (1921-1986) took the symbolism of sheep beyond the page by portraying himself as a shepherd in many of his performance-art pieces. The artist as shepherd became a primary metaphor in Beuy's body of work because it spoke to his belief that the artist is capable of elevating followers to higher insight by leading them to a specific concept or state of mind known only to the artist.

The Green Meadow, 1986, OIL ON MASONITE, GIFT OF THE ESTATE OF JOHN A. AND MARGARET HILL, 1994.19.26

JOHN BAEDER (AMERICAN, B.1938)

Tootsie's Orchid Lounge, 1986 WATERCOLOR, MUSEUM PURCHASE, 1987.5

John Baeder paints meticulously in the manner of the Photo-realists, but unlike them Baeder seeks to imbue the subject matter with a spiritual or metaphysical content. Photo-realists fashioned paintings from photographs to achieve a flattened distortion of reality and with little interest beyond the apparent, observable subject. Their work stands in contradistinction to painting from nature, which is Baeder's principle interest. Baeder's choice of subject also appears similar to the Photo-realists' preference for abject banality. In fact, the opposite is true. Diners, his most well-known subject, are chosen for what Baeder deems their ability to speak in sentimental or ritualistic overtures. *Tootsie's Orchard Lounge* conveys a sense of charm for the famous watering hole, where Opry performers enjoyed breaks between sets at the Old Ryman Auditorium. Using the convenient alley located between the Grand Ole Opry and Tootsie's, singers and musicians made the bar famous with country music fans and tourists who commingled with their favorite stars.

DOUG HOLLIS (AMERICAN, B. 1948)

Doug Hollis's twenty-foot *Windharp Chairs,* constructed from painted steel and piano wire, typify the work that has placed him as one of the pioneers of sound sculpture. The wire creates an aeolian harp that gently hums in the wind, evoking in sound the unseen presence of nature. The chairs' oversized proportions and their placement in a clearing of the sculpture trail create an aura of fantasy reminiscent of Lewis Carroll's *Alice in Wonderland.* Hollis began working with natural phenomena in the late 1960s. His fascination with the integration of sound, sight, and landscape led Hollis to create such well-known, wind-activated works as the *Sound Garden* in Seattle (the inspiration for an alternative rock band), *Sound Site* at Art Park along the Niagara River, and *Field of Vision* for the 1980 Olympic Games in Lake Placid, New York.

High-back Windharp Chairs, 1987, STEEL AND PIANO WIRE, GIFT OF BE&K CONSTRUCTION AND ENGINEERING, INC., BIRMINGHAM, ALABAMA, 1999.1.1-2

ULRICH RÜCKRIEM (GERMAN, B. 1938)

Setting is of central importance for Ulrich Ruckriem's granite forms. Pulled as a raw block from a Yugoslavian quarry before civil unrest forced the artist to quarry in other lands, this monolithic sculpture takes on new meaning within Cheekwood's natural woodland setting. The sculpture's sharp geometric edges contrast with the woodland's curving, organic forms, encouraging viewers to take special notice not only of the sculpture but also of the rich, verdant surroundings. Contrast is found again in the finish of the sculpture's surface. Ruckriem squarely cut two corners of the stone and polished them, producing the contrast with the rough, undulating shapes of the natural rock. He also left the marks created during the quarrying process so that viewers can recreate the history of the sculpture's creation. Although his work is well represented throughout Europe, Ruckriem's sculpture is still rare in America.

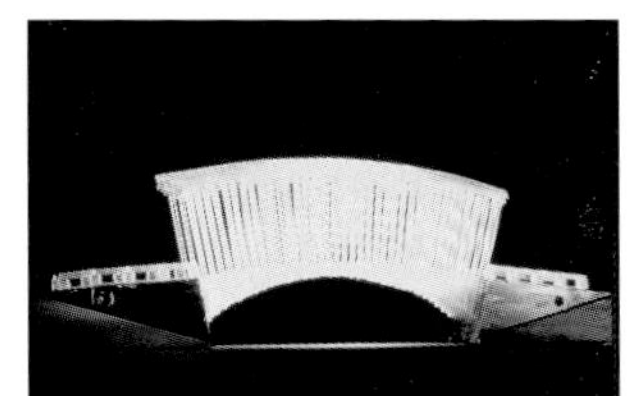

Untitled, 1993,
JUGOSLAVIAN GRANITE,
MUSEUM PURCHASE, 1997.5

TOM CZARNOPYS (AMERICAN, B. 1957)

It is quite possible simply to walk past *Girdled Figure* without recognizing that it is a work of art. Meticulously crafted, the sculpture blends impeccably with its surroundings, appearing at first glance merely to resemble a tree. Upon closer inspection the tree seems to change right before the viewer's eyes, producing a slightly macabre effect–a body materializes. The bronze sculpture seems to change with the seasons: in spring and summer it stands out from the greenery, like a leafless stump; in the fall and winter, it returns to hiding with its cousins, the real trees.

Like Pan the god of the forests and fields and his dryads (wood-nymphs), *Girdled Figure* guards the mysteries of the woods. Dryads were believed to be born and to live in trees, so much a part of nature that they could not be separated from it. It was once considered a sacrilege to destroy a tree carelessly, and punishment was often severe. To girdle a tree means to cut around its base to kill it. *Girdled Figure* anthropomorphizes the tree, dramatically accentuating the preciousness of nature and, with it, human life.

Girdled Figure, 1989,
CAST 1997, BRONZE, MUSEUM
PURCHASE, 1997.2

SIAH ARMAJANI (AMERICAN, B. IRAN 1939)

Siah Armajani's *Glass Bridge* was inspired by Venetian glass blowers of the Renaissance who failed at constructing a glass bridge to span the Grand Canal. Armajani's bridge is at once an engineering tour de force and an object of remarkable beauty. It also functions as a usable pedestrian bridge, creating an active environment for art rather than merely an object for the eyes. Among his most prestigious commissions are the Irene Hixon *Whitney Bridge* in Minneapolis that spans a fourteen-lane highway and leads to the Walker Art Center's sculpture garden, a lighthouse and bridge for Staten Island New York, and the Olympic Torch for the 1996 Games in Atlanta. Armajani has characterized his work as "low, common and close to the people." He describes as his art's purpose "to find a way to make life better and easier for everyone." Yet, for all his modest claims, his art is richly intelligent, learned, and aesthetically sublime.

Glass Bridge (MAQUETTE), 1999,
GLASS, MUSEUM PURCHASE

291 Gallery — 108
Abbott, Berenice — 14, 150
Abstract Expressionism — 72, 155
Abstract Expressionists — 68, 153, 155
Abstraction — 109
Académie Julian — 63, 119, 145-146, 149
Ackerman Foundation, Martin S. — 14
Acklen, Joseph and Adelicia — 143
Adam, Robert — 84, 88, 91
Adelia Boisseau Warfield and Daughter, Huldah Belle, and William Wallace Warfield and Son, [William Laban] — 142
Alcock, Rutherford — 43
Ambiguous Beauty/Aimai-No-Bi — 116
American Academy and Institute of Arts and Letters — 155
Andersen, Hans — 29, 30, 142
Anderson, Sherwood — 112
Animation for "Tappy Toes" — 127
Aravaipa — 27
Armajani, Siah — 157
Armory Show — 40, 64, 120, 146-147
Art Academy of Cincinnati — 145
Art Institute of Chicago — 103, 146-147
Art Nouveau — 96, 112
Art Students League — 47, 67, 71, 108, 111, 145-147, 153
A Sketch of Cliffs in Kaaterskill Clove — 143
Ashcan School — 35, 59, 147
Atget, Eugene — 150
Auden, W. H. — 80
Avedon, Richard — 76
Avent, Mr. and Mrs. James — 28
Baeder, John — 156
Baldaia, Peter — 80
Balink, Henry C. — 145, 152
Barbizon School — 36, 47, 107, 144
Barnes, Dr. Albert C. — 51, 56
Baroque period — 146
Barr, Alfred — 124
Barr, Flight and Barr — 91
Bateman, Hester — 88
Bauhaus school — 120
BE&K Construction and Engineering, Inc — 156
Beal, Jack — 155
Beaman, Alvin G. — 73
Beaman, Mr. and Mrs. Alvin G. — 127
Beard, Tom — 76
Beasley, Mrs. Catherine Ferris — 148
Begay, Harrison — 145
Belasco's Stuyvesant Theater — 104
Bellport Regatta — 57
Belmont — 143
Benson, Frank Weston — 47
Benton, Thomas Hart — 67, 119
Berezov Family — 153
Bernal Foundation of Nashville — 73, 107, 127
Berninghaus, Oscar E. — 149
Bess and Joe — 125, 138 (detail)
Beuys, Joseph — 156
Bishop, Isabel — 14, 71
Bissell, Edgar Julian — 14, 145
Bisttram, Emil — 155
Black Revue from The Boston Massacre — 72

Bloomfield — 148
Blount, Charles — 20
Blue Pesher — 132, 133
Bluemner, Oscar — 148
Blumenschein, Ernest — 145
Bohrod, Aaron — 147
Bonnard, Pierre — 108
Botticelli, Sandro — 40
Bouguereau, Adolph-William — 145, 149
Boulanger, Gustave — 43, 145
Bourdelle, Emile-Antoine — 122
Boys Picking from the *Migrant Workers* essay — 35
Bracque, Georges — 108
Bradford, William — 28
Branchville, CT — 47
Brandt, Grace Borgenicht — 69
Bresson, Henri-Cartier — 80
Bridal Path, Central Park — 104
Bromley, Mrs. Rose M. Formosa — 125
Brown, John George — 32
Brown, Mr. and Mrs. Martin — 73, 91, 127
Brown, Mrs. Martin S. — 91
Brown, William Mason — 27
Buckingham, Duke of — 91
Buckingham, Marquis of — 91
Buntin, Mr. and Mrs. Roger C. — 77-78
Burch, Charles Schiff — 42
Burchfield, Charles — 14, 108, 112
Burkhardt, Tom — 127
Burn, Mrs. Jerry C. — 43
Caldwell, Jr., Dr. and Mrs. Benjamin — 12, 14, 91, 104, 107, 154
Camera Work magazine — 108
Cape Cod School of Art — 64, 148
Carell Woodland Sculpture Trail — 10, 132, 136, 156
Cartwright, Mrs. Robert B. — 119
Castelli, Leo — 76
Centaurs of the Canyon — 153
Century magazine — 36, 40
Ceremonial Beast — 154
Cezanne, Paul — 108, 119
Ch'ing Dynasty — 87
Chamberlain — 91
Champion — 95
Charlotte, Queen — 91
Chase, William Merritt — 14, 44, 60, 64,107, 111, 145, 148, 152
Chattanooga Art Association — 8
Cheat River Gorge — 26
Cheek, Joel — 6
Cheek, Jr., Leslie — 6, 14, 85
Cheek, Jr., Mr. and Mrs. Leslie — 142
Cheek, Mabel Wood — 6,14
Cheek, Sr., Leslie — 6
Cheekwood Collectors' Group — 14, 40, 54, 65, 105, 117, 147
Cheekwood National Contemporary PaintingCompetition — 79, 81
Cheekwood Prime Matter — 137
Ch'ien-lung — 87
Chinoiserie — 91
Chippendale, Thomas — 84, 92
Chowtime in Montana — 67

Chrysler Building Gargoyle — 150
Church, Frederic — 28
Clarence, Duke of — 91
Clark, Barbara Massey — 73
Clark, Mr. and Mrs. George — 45, 112, 127
Clipper Ship Red Jacket — 142
Coggins, Robert P. — 100
Coke Break — 70
Coleman, Michael — 156
Commerce Union Bank — 9
Coney Island — 117
Connally, Mr. and Mrs. John — 14
Cooper Union — 67
Cooper, Washington Bogart — 23, 43, 144
Copley, John Singleton — 20
Copse — 47
Corcoran Gallery of Art — 67, 124
Corregio, Antonio Allegri — 144
Corwine, A. H. — 140
Cos Cob, CT — 47
Couse, Eanger Irving — 145, 149
Cowboy's Day Off — 67
Crane, Stephen — 51
Crawling Lady Hare — 11, 130
Cream Jug — 90
Crepsin, Paul — 95
Cubism — 111, 119-120, 146
Currier, Nathaniel — 142
Curry, John Steuart — 67
Czarnopys, Tom — 157
da Vinci, Leonardo — 115, 116, 144
Dahl-Wolfe, Louise — 10, 14, 115, 124, 151, 153
Danenberg, Bernard — 116
Daniels, Mrs. Josephus — 22
DaPuzzo, Mr. and Mrs. Peter — 38
Davies, Arthur B. — 14, 40, 51
Davies, Virginia Merriweather — 40
Davis, Stuart — 120
de Camp, Joseph — 47
de Kooning, Willem — 68, 72, 155
de Laramie, Paul — 95
De Stijl movement — 120
Degas, Edgar — 100
Delacroix, Eugène — 116
Delano, Gerard Curtis — 153
Delay, Mr. William T. — 90
Delay, Mrs. Wayne T. — 90
Derain, Andre — 103
Dewing, Thomas — 47
Diez, Wilhelm von — 35
Dish — 12, 91
Dixon, Maynard — 150
Dodge, John Wood — 14, 141
Dorothy in Black — 45
Douglas, Ellenna Webb — 120, 150
Dove, Arthur — 108, 148
Dow, Arthur Wesley — 108, 149
du Bois, Guy Péne — 14, 51, 71, 148
Durand-Ruel Gallery — 107
Dutch Masters I — 73
Duveneck, Frank — 14, 35, 43-44, 100, 146
Eagle Console Table — 85
Eakins, Thomas — 79

Earl, Ralph Eleaser Whiteside — 23, 144
Earl, Ralph — 23, 140
Easter Sunday — 43
Edmondson, William — 14, 124, 151-152
Edward VII — 43
Eichholtz, Jacob — 140
Eight, the — 10, 14, 51, 103, 147
El Greco (Domeniko Theotokopoulos) — 119
Elkington and Co. — 95
Elliott, Jr., B. Charles — 8
Emerson, Ralph Waldo — 112, 144
Empire State Building Under Construction — 120
Entrance to the Harbor – Breezy Morning — 30
Entrekin, Mr. and Mrs. Ervin M. — 46, 126
Entry Stone, Cheekwood mansion — 128
Epergne — 12, 94, 95
Ephraim Hubbard Foster — 23
Estes, Jr., Mrs. P. M. — 92
Evans, Walker — 150
Eve — 15, 151
Ewers Acquisition Fund — 91
Ewers, Dr. and Mrs. William — 73, 90, 127
Factory, the — 79
Falconieri Gardens, Frascati — 146
Falls City — 80
Family Gathering — 65
Fauvism — 56, 119, 146
Fine, Perle — 153
Finlay, Ian Hamilton — 10, 128
Fire on Twenty-Fourth Street — 105
First Pacific Railroad — 150
First Period — 91
Fleming, Bryant — 6, 84
Fletcher, John Gould — 55
Flight and Barr — 91
Flight — 91
Flight, Barr and Barr — 91
Flowers with Dogwood — 111
Formosa family — 14
Formosa, Jr., Angelo — 125
Formosa, Sr., Mrs. Pete A. — 125
Formosa, Sr., Salvatore J. — 125
Fort family, Rufus — 14
Foster, Ephraim Hubbard — 22
Foster, Mr. Stratton M. — 23
Fowler, Frank — 76
Fowler, Mr. and Mrs. Frank — 77-78
Fugitives — 124, 151
Fuller, Edmund — 124
Fussell, Valerie — 79
Futurists — 111
Gainsborough, Thomas — 20
Garden of Dreams — 149
Garibaldi, Giuseppe — 103
Gaugin, Paul — 119-120
Genth, Lillian — 14, 52
George III — 88, 90, 91
Gibbes Art Gallery — 8
Gifford, Sanford R. — 143
Girard, William Washington — 146
Girdled Figure — 157
Girl Sleeping — 104
Girl with Cape — 152

Girl with Doves — 41
Girl with Japanese Lanterns — 147
Glackens, William — 14, 48, 51, 56
Glass Bridge (Maquette) — 157
Goodrich, Lloyd — 116
Gore, Sr., Senator Albert — 8
Gorky, Arshile — 153
Gothic House — 112
Goya, Francisco — 131
Griffin, Walter — 107
Grogan, Kevin — 10
Grooms, Charles (Red) — 72, 127
Guggenheim Museum — 75
Guy, Seymour — 32
Hale, Dr. and Mrs. George W. — 27
Hals, Frans — 35
Halsman, Philippe — 14
Hamilton, James — 28
Hammer, Dr. and Mrs. Armand — 62
Hankins, Cornelius — 14
Harper's Bazaar magazine — 40, 115, 124
Harwell, Anne Howe — 141
Hassam and Speicher Purchase Fund — 155
Hassam, Childe — 14, 47, 60, 63, 103, 107
Hawthorne, Charles — 64, 148
Hayes and Co., Inc., Martin — 77-78
Heermann, Norbert — 35
Henri, Robert — 14, 35-36, 51, 56, 59, 71, 103, 112, 120, 148
Hergesheimer, Ella Sophonisba — 14, 52, 152
Hicks, Edward — 141
Hicks, Thomas — 141
High Museum of Art — 154
High-back Windharp Chairs — 156
Hill, John A. and Margaret — 27, 59, 66, 67, 118, 147, 149-150, 152, 153, 155-156
Hill, Mary Cheek — 10
Hirsch, Sidney Mttron — 124, 151
His First Vote — 33
Hofmann, Hans — 68, 153
Holbein, Hans — 144
Hollis, Doug — 11, 156
Holzer, Jenny — 75
Homer, Winslow — 60, 79
Hopps, Walter — 79
Horticulture Society of Davidson County — 7
Howell, Mamie C. — 77-78
Howell, Nancy W. — 20
Hudson River School — 27-28, 36, 112, 146
Hughes, Robert — 132
Huneker, James G. — 51
Hunt & Company, John — 95
Hunt and Roskell — 95
Hunt, William Morris — 144
Hurrell, George — 14
Idyllic Landscape — 40
Impressionism — 32, 44, 63-64, 100, 107, 148
Impressionist — 47, 51, 52, 63, 64, 68, 103, 107-108, 148-149
Inman, Henry — 144
Inness, George — 14, 36, 96
Is He Home? — 104
Italian Renaissance — 84

Ives, James Merritt — 142
Jackson, Andrew — 23, 140, 144
James, Henry — 51
James, Jr. Dr. A. Everette — 64, 148
Jefferson, Thomas — 92
Jimmy — 49
Johansen, John Christen — 146
Johns, Jasper — 72
Johnson, Eastman — 14, 144
Johnson, Harvey — 67
Johnson, Mr. and Mrs. D. W. — 73, 127
Jones, Inigo — 84
Juan — 59
Judd, Mr. and Mrs. Eugene — 68
June, Mr. and Mrs. O. W. — 93
Kahn, Wolf — 47
Kanaf, Naomi M. — 143
Kandinsky, Wassily — 108, 148
Kathleen Millay — 110
Kennington, Dale — 80
Kent, Rockwell — 51
Key, Mr. and Mrs. Martin B. — 144
Kneehole Desk — 92
Knestrick, Mr. and Mrs. Walter — 14, 20-21, 24-25, 36-37, 44, 47-48, 100, 103-104, 112-113, 126, 140, 143-144, 146-147
Knowles, Susan — 10
Kohlmeyer, Ida — 155
Kroll, Leon — 147
Kruger, Barbara — 76
Lady in White — 47
Landscape in Waterford, Connecticut — 106
Landscape with Two Indians — 27
Lane, Fitz Hugh — 60
Lawrence, Jacob — 32
Lawson, Ernest — 14, 51
Lebeck, Michael — 151
Lefebvre, Jules-Joseph — 43, 145
Leger, Ferdinand — 120
Lewyn, Thomas — 40
Lichtenstein, Roy — 120, 155
Life magazine — 154
Lion passant — 88
London Goldsmiths Hall — 88
Lorillard Company — 32
Louis, Milton — 155
Lowe, Harry — 8, 14
Lucas, Mr. and Mrs. Fred F. — 26
Luks, George — 14, 35, 48, 51, 59, 147
MacBeth Gallery — 51, 103
MacBeth, Russell — 8
Magasins du Bon Marché — 150
Magritte, Réne — 80
Marin, John — 108
Marsh, Reginald — 71, 116
Mason, Allen O. and Elizabeth C. — 97
Massey, Mr. and Mrs. Jack C. — 45, 77-78, 112
Matisse, Henri — 56, 115, 120
Maurer, Alfred — 14, 56
Maxwell House Coffee — 6
McClure's magazine — 145
McCrea, Henriette A. — 107
McGhee, Ms. Tennie — 95

Meat Platter 91
Meissen 91
Metcalf, Willard 47, 107
Metropolitan Life Tower 55
Michelangelo Buonarroti 116
Mienzinger Art School 154
Millay, Edna St. Vincent 111
Miller, Kenneth Hayes 71, 148
Milton on the Hudson 37
Miss Lillian 76
Monet, Claude 63, 68
Moonlit Landscape 146
Moore, Henry 131, 156
Morgan, Barbara 14
Morimura, Yasumasa 116
Morrice, James Wilson 103
Morse, Samuel F. B. 14, 140
Mountain Landscape 103
Mr. and Mrs. Rembrandt 15, 126
Mrs. Ramsey, Gatlinburg, Tennessee 114
Muir, John 112
Munich Royal Academy 35, 44
Museum of Fine Arts, Boston 8
Museum of Modern Art 75, 124, 151
Nashville Art Association 8
Nashville Artists' Guild 9
Nashville Banner newspaper 43
Nashville Exchange Club Charities 7, 73, 112, 127, 155
Nashville Museum of Art 7-8, 12, 14, 27, 42, 52-53, 60,141, 144-145, 149, 152
Nashville, TN 23,32,154
National Academy of Design 28, 32, 43, 51, 96, 140-141,146, 147, 149
National Endowment for the Arts 73, 127
Nederlander, Mr. Fred 154
Neuhaus, Robert 35
New York City 60, 149, 155
New York in the Snow 147
New York School of Applied Design for Women 71
New York School of Art 68, 111, 148, 153
New York University 140
Newman, Robert Loftin 142, 144
Newman, Willie Betty 145
Newsweek magazine 154
Night Bathing 63, 153
NLT Corporation 77-78
Noland, Kenneth 10, 155
Norton Family, Peter 116
Nozynski, John 8, 9
Nude 63
Nudo 108
O'Keeffe, Georgia 44, 108, 148, 155
Oakland Art Museum 8
Old Lyme, CT 47, 107
Oldham, Dortch 73
Oldham, Mr. and Mrs. Dortch 127
Oliver, Corinne Craig 77-78
Oman, Jr., Mr. and Mrs. John 77-78
On the Aegean Sea 127
On the Roof 148
Orchard 101
Orr, Eric 11, 136
Pair of Gardners 95

Palladio, Andrea 84
Palmer, Pauline 64
Peale, Charles Willson 24, 152
Peale, James 14, 24
Peale, Rembrandt 14, 24
Pendleton, Dr. G.T. 141
Péne du Bois, Guy 148
Penelope 39, 122 (detail)
Pennsylvania Academy of the Fine Arts 43, 52, 56, 60, 108, 141, 144
Philadelphia Press newspaper 120
Phillips Collection 10
Phillips, Bert 145
Photo-realists 156
Picasso, Pablo 108, 131
Pigeons Flying 112
Pinkstone 68
Piranesi, Giovanni Battista 84
Plate 82, 91
Plowing It Under 119
Pointillist movement 103, 107
Pollock, Jackson 68, 72, 153
Pop Art 72, 120, 127
Portrait of a Lady with Lace Collar 141
Portrait of a Man 25
Portrait of a Student 64
Portrait of an Unknown Gentleman (possibly General Pierson) 20
Portrait of Andrew Jackson 140
Portrait of Andy Warhol 78
Portrait of Brigadier Robert Coleman Foster 23
Portrait of Elizabeth O'Nora Yaeger 141
Portrait of George Washington 20
Portrait of Jacob Barge Weidman 140
Portrait of Jamie Wyeth with Tan Background 77
Portrait of John Henry Twachtman 100
Portrait of Judge Trimble 24
Portrait of Little Bear 152
Portrait of Mrs. N. Lansing Zabriskie 44
Portrait of Robert Henri 56
Portrait of Stephen J. Breslin 48
Portrait of the Artist's Brother 140
Portrait of the Schiff Children 42
Portrait of William McCracken 21
Posthumous Likeness of Felix Grundy Eakin 141
Postimpressionist movement 119-120
Prendergast, Maurice 14, 51, 60, 103
Protomaterialist 136
Provincetown 64, 148
Pure Myth 153
Quinn, Dr. and Mrs. Robert 73, 127
Rainbow, New York City 54
Rainey, Ada 52
Rainey, Sue 28
Ranchos Church 155
Ranger, Henry Ward 107
Ransom, John Crowe 151
Raphael Sanzio 144
Rauschenberg, Robert 72
Ray, Man 108
Realism 20, 35, 140, 155
Reclining Man 151
Reed, John 51

Regionalists 67, 71, 147
Reid, Robert 47
Rembrandt van Rijin 35, 40, 72, 127
Remington, Frederic 150
Renaissance 71, 95, 111, 115, 119, 157
Renoir, August 56
Resnick, Milton 68
Reynolds, Sir Joshua 20, 24
Rickey, George 10, 155
Riley, Kenneth 27
Rising Wolf 145
Rivera, Diego 155
Rivers, Larry 72
Robinson, Theodore 47
Rococo period 84, 88, 144
Rogers, Mr. and Mrs. Joe M. 77
Roofs, Summer Night 55
Roosevelt, Franklin D. 119
Rosenblum, Robert 76
Rosenstein, Harris 68
Rotunda at Cheekwood 84
Royal Academy of Arts 28
Rubens, Peter Paul 116, 144
Ruckriem, Ulrich 10, 157
Rudberg, Jay 35
Russell, Charles 149
Ryder, Sophie 11, 131
Ryman, Robert 10, 75
Sadler, Mr. and Mrs. Harry 141
Sailor Girl 60
Saint Louis School of Fine Art 145
Saint-Just, Louis de 128
San Francisco Examiner 150
Sarah, Sally, Sadie, Peter and Paul 55
Saret, Alan 8
Sargent, John Singer 14, 43-44, 60, 146
Sawyer, Bill 80
Scene in Norway 107
Schematic drawings for *Blue Pesher* 132
Schille, Alice 43
Scholder, Fritz 145
School of the Fine Arts in Boston 107
Scott, Harry 131
Scott, John 11, 135
Scout of the Caravan 149
Scribners magazine 40
Seitz, William 68
Self-Portrait 20, 148, 151
Self-Portrait, Flanders 79
Service Merchandise–Zimmerman Family Foundation 79, 81
Set of Four Hinged Medicine Bottle 86
Sevres 91
Shakespeare, Richard 143
Sharp, Mr. and Mrs. Walter 14
Sharp, Mrs. Walter (Huldah Cheek) 6, 7, 12, 80, 92, 94, 144
Sharp, Walter 7-8, 12, 14
Sheraton, Thomas 84, 92
Shinn, Everett 14, 35, 51, 104, 147
Ships Along the Coast 31
Sideboard 92, 93
Signac, Paul 103, 108

Silva, William Posey   149
Simmons, Edward   47
Simpkins, Mr. and Mrs. Irby   145
Slender Trees and Green Leaves   36
Sloan, John   14, 35, 51, 55, 59, 80, 145, 147
Smith, W. Eugene   14, 35, 154
Smithsonian Institution   8, 154
Snuff Bottle   15, 87
Social Realism   148
Society of American Artists   47, 107
Society of Painters in Pastel   100
Soda and Sandwich from the
   Ten Works by Ten Painters Portfolio   120
Sohacki, S.D.   72
Speights, Mr. and Mrs. Russell   14, 88
Sports Illustrated magazine   115
Spring Scene   51
St. Louis School of Fine Arts   149
Stallworth, Mrs. Hugh (Anita Bevill McMichael)
    10, 14, 32-33, 34, 40-41, 44, 49,
    50, 54-58, 60-61, 65, 72,77-78,
    79, 81, 95, 101-102, 105-106,
    108-110,117, 125, 127, 147
Stamps, Mr. and Mrs. John   45, 112
Starr family   124
Starr, Alfred   151
Starr, Mrs. Alfred (Elizabeth Lyle)   14, 151, 152
Steger, Mrs. Nannie Eakin   141
Stein family   56
Stein, Gertrude   56
Steine, David   45, 112
Stella, Joseph   44, 111
Stella, Sergio   111
Stengel, Mrs. Sara S.   127
Stieglitz, Alfred   56, 108
Still Life with Snow Shovel   155
Storr, Paul   95
Story, Julian   14, 43
Stowe Service   90, 91
Stowe Tureen   90
Strand, Paul   108
Street & Street   8
Street Scene   48
Stuart, Gilbert   20, 140
Study for *Coke Break*   71
Study for *Dutch Masters*   72
Study for *The Boy*   118
Style   81
Sully, Thomas   14, 140, 144
Summer Afternoon   12, 53
Sunset in the Arctic   15, 29
Surrealism   80
Svenson, Sven   28
Swan Ball Patrons   41, 127
Swendenborg, Emanuel   36
Symbols 81-5   155
Symond, Susan   140
Synchronism   119
Tarbell, Edmund   47
Tate, Allen   151
Teapot   88, 91
Tea Service   88 (detail), 89
Ten, the   47, 107

Tennessee Association of Museums   10
Tennessee State Museum   124
Tennessee   8, 92, 115, 124, 142, 144-146, 149
Tenth Street Studio   32, 44
Texas John Kelly   66
The 1920's – The Migrants Cast Their Ballots   32
The Blacksmith Shop   144
The Blue Jar   52
The Dead Trees   113
The Ephraim Hubbard Foster Family   13, 22
The Failure of Sylvester   16, 58
The Fire Maker   149
The Frugal Repast   145
The Green Meadow   156
The Humorist - Whiskey and Soda   145
The Keith Children   144
The Old Navy Yard   31
The Order of the Present is the Disorder of the Future –
   Saint Just   129
The Pantheon   84
The Sapphire Slipper   32
The Smoker - Portrait of Frank Duveneck   44
The Story Book   146
The Thomas Foster Family   43
The Whistling Boy   34
The Witching Hour   144
Thomas, Dylan   100
Thompson, Mr. and Mrs. Joseph H.   12, 14
Thompson, Mrs. Joseph   86-87
Thoreau, Henry David   27
Thruston, General Gates P.   12
Tiffany & Co.   96
Tiffany, Charles L.   96
Tiffany, Louis Comfort   96
Time magazine   132
Titian (Tiziano Vecelli)   20, 144
Tonalism   149
Tootsie's Orchid Lounge   156
Top of Cape Ann Spring   62
Toward Union Pleased   68
Tree Poem   134
Trumball, John   20
Trumpet Vase   97
Turrell, James   11, 132
Twachtman, John Henry   47, 51, 100, 107, 147
Two Figures in a Landscape   40
Tyne, Mrs. William J.   10, 95
University of Virginia   149
University of Wisconsin   67
Untitled   18 (detail), 69, 98 (detail), 107, 157
Untitled (Dutch Boy Diamond #5)   74
Untitled (In a Dream)   75
Untitled from the *Pittsburgh* essay   154
Untitled (landscape)   100
Untitled from the
   Ten Works by Ten Painters portfolio   121
Upper Broadway   147
Urban Realists   59
van Beest, Albert   28
Van Dyck, Anthony   20, 144
Van Gogh, Vincent   120
Van Soelen, Theodore   67
Vanderbilt University   124, 151

Vanity Fair magazine   115
Vedder, Elihu   63
Velázquez, Diego Rodriguez   35
Veronese (Pablo Cagliari)   144
Via Garibaldi   102
Victoria, Queen   28
View of Segovia   51
Vogue magazine   115
Wadsworth Athenaeum   120
Wall, Dr.   91
Walter Sharp Distinguished Lectureship   8
Walter Sharp Memorial Fund   104
Walter, Martha   52, 60
Ward, Jr., Mr. Newell J.   140
Warhol, Andy   9, 76, 79
Warren, Robert Penn   151
Washington Square   50
Washington, George   20, 24, 51
Waterford   107
Webb, A. C.   120, 150
Weir, John Ferguson   47
Weir, Julian Alden   14, 47, 51, 107
Weir, Robert W.   47
Wells, Dr. and Mrs. Charles E.   70, 73, 127
Werthan Family Foundation   127
Werthan, Mr. and Mrs. Albert   45, 112
West, Benjamin   20, 24
Wetenhall, Dr. John   10
Whistler, James Abbott McNeil   43, 44, 52, 100,
    103,108, 146
White, Stanford   51, 104
Whitney, Gertrude Vanderbilt   51
Whitney, Mrs. Harry Paine   67
Whittemore, William John   60
Who Wins May Wear   38
Wildner, Werner   154
Windy Day by the Sea   61
Winter Landscape   28, 46
Wolfe, Meyer   14
Wood, Grant   67
Wood, Thomas Waterman   32
Woosley, Mrs. Lula   89
Worcester porcelain   10, 91
Works Progress Administration   67
Wren, Sir Christopher   7, 84
Wunderlich Gallery   100
Wyeth, Andrew   79
Wyeth, James (Jamie)   9, 76, 79
Wyler, Seymour B.   88
Yorkshire Sculpture Park   131